The Krishnamurti Reader

BOOKS BY J. KRISHNAMURTI

Can Humanity Change?:
J. Krishnamurti in Dialogue with Buddhists

Facing a World in Crisis:
What Life Teaches Us in Challenging Times

Freedom, Love, and Action

Inward Revolution:
Bringing about Radical Change in the World

Meditations

Talks with American Students

This Light in Oneself: True Meditation

Where Can Peace Be Found?

THE
Krishnamurti Reader

J. Krishnamurti

SHAMBHALA
Boston & London
2011

Shambhala Publications, Inc.
Horticultural Hall
300 Massachusetts Avenue
Boston, Massachusetts 02115
www.shambhala.com

©2009 by Krishnamurti Foundation Trust, Ltd
Brockwood Park, Bramdean Hampshire so24 0LQ England
info@brockwood.org.uk, www.kfoundation.org
This book was previously published as *The Pocket Krishnamurti*.

Edited by Ray McCoy

9 8 7 6 5 4 3 2

Printed in USA

⊗This edition is printed on acid-free paper that meets the
American National Standards Institute z39.48 Standard.
♻This book is printed on 100% recycled paper.
For more information please visit www.shambhala.com

Distributed in the United States by Random House, Inc.,
and in Canada by Random House of Canada Ltd

Designed by James D. Skatges

Library of Congress Cataloging-in-Publication Data
Krishnamurti, J. (Jiddu), 1895–1986.
[Selections. 2011]
The Krishnamurti reader / J. Krishnamurti—1st ed.
p. cm.
ISBN 978-1-59030-938-4 (pbk.: alk. paper)
1. Hindu philosophy. I. title
B5134.K752E5 2011
181'.4—DC22

CONTENTS

Contents

EDITOR'S INTRODUCTION

The Art of Living

DO WE SOMETIMES FEEL that we waste our lives, that they are without meaning, full of conflict and confusion around us and within us? In this collection, comprised mostly of unpublished talks given in California, England, and Switzerland, Krishnamurti considers these feelings, and suggests that there is a way of living daily life that is entirely different from what it normally is—a way of living without any control, without any conflict, yet without conformity. He says that life can have great beauty and significance if there is clear observation of what is actually happening in our actions and reactions, in our relationships. Human beings have tremendous capacity but we are conditioned to solve problems; this denies freedom. When we recognize our conditioning, Krishnamurti explains, we reject psychological authority, and may then observe and act with greater clarity. With observation free of words and thought, we can see that freedom, love, beauty, and goodness are one, not separate.

Krishnamurti speaks of an art of living a life in which there is no conflict whatsoever, one that is totally free of fear, including the fear of death. We can understand the root of fear and the cause of sorrow if we look at our conditioning. In this way we see that thought is a process of time and memory that interferes with direct perception. Understanding what prevents order in consciousness, and so in our lives, depends on the arts of listening, seeing, and learning. Krishnamurti discusses each of these in simple words with the freshness of truth.

In these talks, which Krishnamurti described as conversations between us and him, there is a quality of meditation in which we may glimpse a timeless emptiness that is, perhaps, sacred, with meaning beyond words.

RAY McCOY

The Krishnamurti Reader

I

Life Is What Is Happening This Instant

THE GREATEST ART is the art of living, greater than all things that human beings have created by mind or hand, greater than all the scriptures and their gods. It is only through this art of living that a new culture can come into being. This art of living can come only out of total freedom.

This freedom is not an ideal, a thing to take place eventually. The first step in freedom is the last step in it. It is the first step that counts, not the last step. What you do now is far more essential than what you do at some future date. Life is what is happening this instant, not an imagined instant, not what thought has conceived, so it is the first step you take now that is important. If that step is in the right direction, then the whole of life is open to you. The right direction is not toward an ideal, a predetermined end, it is inseparable from what is taking place now. This is not a philosophy as a series of theories; it is exactly what the word philosophy means, the love of truth, the love of life. It is not something that you go to a university to learn. We are learning about the art of living in our daily life.

As life is so complex, it is always difficult and confusing to pick one aspect and say it is the most important. The very choice, the differentiating quality, leads to further confusion. If you say this is the most important, then you relegate the other facts of life to a secondary position. Either we take the whole movement of life as one, which becomes extremely difficult for most people, or we take one fundamental aspect in which all the others may be included. Let us go into it very slowly and hesitantly.

We are exploring together one facet of life, and in the very understanding of it we may cover the whole field of life. To investigate, we must be free of our prejudices, personal experiences, and pre-determined conclusions. Like a good scientist, we must have a mind unclouded by knowledge that we have already accumulated. We must come to it afresh, without any reaction to what is being observed. This is absolutely necessary; otherwise investigation is colored by our own fears, hopes, and pleasures. The very urge to investigate, and the intensity of it, frees the mind from its coloring.

One of the most important things is the art of living. Is there a way of living our daily life that is entirely different from what it normally is? Is there a way of living without any control, without any conflict, without a disciplinary conformity? I can find out only when my whole mind is facing exactly what is happening now. This means I can find out what it means to live without conflict only when what is happening *now* can be observed.

This observation is not an intellectual or emotional affair but acute, clear, sharp perception in which there is no duality, no opposition or contradiction in what is going on. Duality arises only when there is an escape from *what is*. This escape creates the opposite and so conflict arises. There is only the actual and nothing else.

Associations and reactions to what is happening are the conditioning of the mind. This conditioning prevents the observation of what is taking place now. What is taking place now is free of time. Time is the evolution of our conditioning. It is humanity's inheritance, the burden that has no beginning. When there is this passionate observation of what is going on, that which is being observed dissolves into nothingness. An observation of anger that is taking place now reveals the whole nature and structure of violence. This insight is the ending of all violence.

Anger has many stories behind it. It is not just a solitary event. It has a great many associations. These very associations, with their emotions, prevent actual observation. With anger the content is the anger. The anger is the content; they are not two separate things. The content is the conditioning. In the passionate observation of what is actually going on—that is, of the activities of the conditioning—the nature and structure of the conditioning are dissolved.

It is really simple, so simple that you miss its very simplicity and so its subtlety. What we are saying is that whatever is happening, when you are walking, talking, meditating, the event that is taking place is to be observed. When the mind wanders, the very observation of it ends its chatter. So there is no distraction whatsoever at any time.

Remembrance has no place in the art of living. Relationship is the art of living. If there is remembrance in relationship, it is not relationship. Relationship is between human beings, not their memories. It is these memories that divide, and so there is contention, the opposition of the "you" and the "me." So thought, which is remembrance, has no place whatsoever in relationship. This is the art of living.

Relationship is to all things, to nature, the birds, the rocks—to everything around us and above us—to the clouds, the stars, and the blue sky. All existence is relationship; without it you cannot live. Because we have corrupted relationship, we live in a society that is degenerating.

The art of living can come into being only when thought does not contaminate love.

What Do We Want?

I WONDER IF YOU have ever considered how we waste our life, how we dissipate our energies, how intellectually we are secondhand people. There is nothing but routine, boredom, loneliness, suffering, either physiologically or psychologically. Our life, as it is lived now, unfortunately has no meaning whatsoever, except to earn a livelihood, which is obviously necessary. Besides that, our whole life is fragmented, broken up, and a mind that is broken up, fragmented, is a corrupt mind. The word *corrupt* means broken up.

What is it that we want? What is it that we have achieved? What is it that we have become? For most of us, life is travail, strife. In this particular society, to be successful in it is to make money. We are either seeking power, position, prestige, or living a bourgeois, narrow, shallow, empty life, filled with all kinds of opinions, judgments, beliefs. All that seems such a wasteful life. We are never happy except in the pursuit of pleasure, from which we derive a certain sense of enjoyment, a certain sense of gratification, satisfaction. But when you examine a little more deeply into yourself, apart from what you have learned from books, and from the reactions of the country in which you live, don't you find that there is absolutely nothing inward except what you have put into it? What you have put into it is the fabrication of thought. And thought does not bring about the total action of a human being. It is only a partial, fragmentary action.

Realizing that our life, as it is, is empty, rather shallow, and sorrowful, we escape into various pursuits of pleasure, religious pleasure or so-called worldly pleasure, seeking money, greater enjoyment, greater pleasures, buying more things, maintaining a society of consumerism and ultimately ending in the grave. That is our life, and there is nothing sacred, there is nothing really religious.

Life is dreadfully serious, and it is only those who are really deeply serious who *live*. Those who are flippant seek the entertainment of the gurus or the priests, or the intellectual philosophers, and *they* become our life through words without substance, descriptions without the described.

So one asks: what is the place of thought in our life? All our civilization, our culture, is based on thought. Religions are the product of thought; behavior, conduct, the business world, relationship, the accumulation of armaments, the army, the navy, the air force are all based on thought. Whether the thought is reasonable or unreasonable, logical or illogical, sane or neurotic, our action is based on thought as an idea, thought as an ideal. We are all terribly idealistic, most unfortunately. The ideal is not *what is;* the ideal is something invented by thought as a means to overcome *what is*. There is division between that ideal and *what is,* and so, conflict.

I hope you are not merely hearing a series of words but actually observing the whole movement of your own mind so that we can establish a relationship, a communication in which we understand what we are talking about, without agreement or disagreement but merely observing what actually is.

One must go into what thought is and what thinking is. You know, it is one of the most extraordinary things that the whole of Asia considers thought to be the child of a barren woman. They say thought is measure, and to find the immeasurable, that which is beyond time and measure, one must pursue the suppression of thought. Whereas the whole of Western civilization, culture, is based on thought. Thought is measurement.

As I said, this is really very serious, and it requires great subtlety of mind to go into it. I hope you are prepared to investigate this so that the mind is free from measurement, so that the mind knows vast space and silence, which is not measurable, which is not put together by thought.

We are saying that the culture of Western civilization is based on thought, on measurement. From that measurement has grown the whole technological world and the art of war; and in that world, religion is a matter of belief, acceptance, propaganda, saviors, and so on. In the East they use thought to go beyond thought, and in the West they have accepted measurement, progress, and a way of life that is based on technology, acquiring more and more enjoyment, and having great pleasure in possessions, including literature and poetry.

A serious mind must ask what place thought has in life. What is the function of thought, thought that is either sane, logical, reasoned; or that has perverted life, giving importance to *things*, to property, to money, to pleasure; thought, which has accumulated so much information, both outwardly and inwardly? What is the place of thought and what is its relationship to action? Because life is action; relationship is movement in action. Is there an action in life that is not bound by time and thought and measure?

To live is to act. Whatever we do is action, and if that action is bound by the past through the present to the future, then action is never liberating, then action is always fragmentary. And such action is corruption.

So what is action, and what is its relationship to thought? Thought is the response of memory, as knowledge and experience, stored in the brain. You don't have to read neurological or scientific books, you can observe it in yourself if you are deeply interested in it. Without memory you cannot act, you cannot remember words; you then become in a state of amnesia, complete confusion. And thought responds to any challenge according to its conditioning. If you are a Christian or a Hindu or a Buddhist or a communist or a capitalist, your mind is conditioned in that, and you act according to that conditioning. That conditioning is the memory, the experience, the knowledge of that particular culture or society in which you live. That is fairly obvious, isn't it? So thought in action is separative, fragmentary, and brings about conflict.

We must understand this, because we are trying to find a way of life in which there is no conflict whatsoever, a way of life in which there is no sorrow, a way of life that is total, complete, whole, harmonious, sane. And thought may be one of the factors that brings about fragmentation and therefore corruption. Therefore one must find out what the function of thought is and what place thought has in human relationship.

One can see very clearly that thought in the field of technology is essential. In the field of knowledge, thought can function logically, sanely, objectively, efficiently. But that efficiency, sanity, objectivity becomes polluted when thought seeks status through technology. When the mind seeks status through technological function, then inevitably there must be conflict and therefore corruption. That is obvious. But your conditioning is so strong that you will pursue status in spite of logical, sane, rational thinking. You will pursue status, and therefore continue with conflict and therefore corruption. Corruption is not merely taking money from another, or doing ugly things; the deep cause of corruption is when thought breaks up action into fragments—intellectual action, emotional action, physical action, or ideological action.

So, is there an action in human relationship that is not fragmentary but whole? Is there an action that is not controlled by thought or by measurement or by the past? Action is also when you say a word, when you make a gesture of contempt or of welcome; action may be going from here to there. There is action according to a formula, action according to an opinion, action according to an idea, an ideal, or action based on some neurotic or rational belief. It is either acting according to a past pattern, or acting according to a future abstraction.

The most fundamental thing in life is relationship. Behavior, virtue, conduct, and society are born from relationship. And thought is measurement, conformity, acting according to a particular conclusion, from knowledge that is always in the past. What place has thought in human relationship? Or has it no place at all? If it has a place in human relationship, then thought limits, controls relationship, and therefore in that relationship there is fragmentation and hence conflict.

There are two principles on which our life is based: pleasure and fear. Please observe it in yourself. Pleasure has become tremendously important in life. There are various forms of pleasure: sexual pleasure, intellectual pleasure, the pleasure of possession, the pleasure of money, the pleasure of power, prestige, the pleasure of self-importance, the pleasure that you derive when the "me," the ego, asserts itself through domination and so on, or accepts tyranny as a means of achievement. And in relationship, pleasure takes the form of dependency. You depend on another psychologically in relationship. Where there is dependence there must be fear of losing, and therefore greater attachment. The pursuit of pleasure sexually is fairly obvious. Most extraordinarily, this pleasure has become the most important thing in life. There is the pleasure of dependence, depending on another psychologically because in oneself one is frightened of being alone, is lonely, desperate, not having love or not being loved, and so on. So there is the pursuit of pleasure and the constant avoidance of fear. And thought sustains both: you think about the pleasure that you have had yesterday, and you hope to have it again today. And if that pleasure is not continued, you get violent, anxious, fearful. Observe this in yourself.

And there is the whole question of fear. A life that is lived in fear is a dark, ugly life. Most of us are frightened in different ways. Can the mind be totally free of fear? Nobody wants to be free of pleasure but you all want to be free of fear; you don't see that both of them go together, that they are two sides of the same coin, sustained by thought. That is why it is very important to understand thought. You know we have fears: fear of death, fear of life, fear of darkness, fear of our neighbor, fear of ourself, fear of losing a job, and the deeper unconscious layers of fear hidden in the deep recesses of our own mind. There is insecurity and so, seeking security. Is it possible for the mind to be free of fear totally, so the mind is really free to enjoy life—not to pursue pleasure but to enjoy life? It is not possible to enjoy life as long as fear exists.

Will analysis dispel fear? Or is analysis a form of paralyzing the mind not to have freedom from fear? See the implication of it. You are used to analysis; that is one of the intellectual forms of entertainment. In analysis, there is the analyzer and the analyzed, whether the analyzer is a professional or you. When there is analysis, there is division between the analyzer and the analyzed, and hence conflict. And in analysis you need time; you take days, years, and that gives you an opportunity to postpone action. You can analyze the whole problem of violence indefinitely, seeking its cause, hearing the explanations of different professionals about what the causes of violence are, reading volumes about the causes of violence and analyzing them. All that takes time, and in the meantime you can enjoy your violence. Analysis implies division and postponement of action—and therefore analysis brings more conflict, not less. Analysis implies time.

A mind that observes the truth of this is free of analysis, and therefore is capable of directly dealing with violence, which is *what is*. If you observe totally, without analysis, violence in yourself—violence brought about through fear, through insecurity, through the sense of loneliness, dependency, through the cutting off of your pleasures, and so on—then you have all the energy that has been dissipated through analysis to go beyond *what is*.

Can the deep-rooted fears given to us by the society in which we live, inherited from the past, all be exposed so that the mind is completely free of this terrible thing called fear? Can one observe the totality of fear, or only the branches of fear, not the very root of fear, the cause of fear? Can the mind observe, see, be aware of, give total attention to fear, whether it is hidden, put away deeply in the recesses of one's own mind, or seen in the outward expressions of daily fears—like the fear of the pain of yesterday coming back again today or tomorrow? The fear of losing a job, the fear of being insecure outwardly as well as inwardly, the ultimate fear of death—there are so many forms of fear. Should we cut away each branch or come to grips with the totality of fear? Is the mind capable of observing fear totally?

We are used to dealing with fear in fragments. I am afraid of this or that; I am afraid of losing a job, or afraid of my wife, or my husband; I am concerned with fragments and not with the totality of fear. To observe the totality of fear is to give complete attention when any fear arises.

You know, we look at anger or jealousy, envy, fear, or pleasure as an observer wanting to get rid of it. There is always an observer, a seer, a thinker, so we look at fear as though we were outside looking in. Now, can you observe fear without the observer? The observer is the past. The observer recognizes the reaction that it calls *fear* in terms of the past, and names it as fear. The observer is always looking from the past at the present, and so there is a division between the observer and the observed. Can you observe fear without the reaction to that as the past, which is the observer?

Look, I have met you in the past and you have insulted me, flattered me. You have done a great many things for me and against me. All that is the accumulated memory that is the past. The past is the observer, is the thinker, and when he or she looks at you, he or she is looking with the eyes of the past and does not look at you afresh. So the observer never sees you properly, he or she only sees you with the eyes that have already been corrupted, that have already been dulled. So can you observe fear without the past? That means not to name the fear, not to use the word *fear* at all, but just to observe. That totality of attention is possible only when there is no observer, which is the past. When you do that, when you observe totally, then the whole content of consciousness as fear is dissipated.

There is fear from outside and from within. I fear that my son may get killed in a war. War is external, the invention of technology, which has developed such monstrous instruments of destruction. Inwardly I cling to my son; I love him, and I have educated him to conform to the society in which he lives, which says to kill. We have built a society that is so corrupt, that is so immoral. It is concerned only with possessing more and more, with consumerism. It is not concerned with the total development of the world, of human beings.

You know, we have no compassion. We have a great deal of knowledge, a great deal of experience. We can do extraordinary things medically, technologically, scientifically, but we have no compassion whatsoever. Compassion means passion for all human beings, and animals, nature. How can there be compassion when there is fear, when the mind is constantly pursuing pleasure? You want pleasure; you want to control fear, put it underground; and you also want compassion. You want it all, but you cannot have it. You can have compassion only when fear is not. And that is why it is so important to understand fear in our relationship. That fear can be totally uprooted when you can observe the reaction without naming it. The very naming of it is the projection of the past. So thought sustains and pursues pleasure, and thought also gives strength to fear—I am afraid of what might happen tomorrow, I am afraid of losing a job, I am afraid of time as death.

So thought is responsible for fear. And we live in thought, our daily activity is based on thought. What place has thought in human relationship? You have insulted me; that leaves a memory, that leaves a mark as memory in my mind, and I look at you with that memory. Or if you flatter me, I look at you with that memory. So I have never looked at you without the eyes of the past. So it is very important to understand what place thought has in relationship. If it has a place, then relationship is daily routine, mechanical, with meaningless pleasure and fear.

Then one comes to the question: what is love? Is it the product of thought? Unfortunately it has been made the product of thought—we "love" God and "love" man— and destroy nature. One must go into this question deeply to find out for oneself what love is, because without that, without that quality of compassion, we will always suffer. And to come upon it, for the mind to have that deep compassion, one must understand suffering, for passion is the outcome of suffering. The root meaning of the word *passion* is sorrow, suffering; and most of us escape from suffering. It is not that we must accept physical and psychological suffering. That is silly. But is thought the movement of suffering? Or is suffering something entirely different from thought? It is immensely important to understand the machinery of thinking, not verbally understand it but actually observe in ourselves what thinking is, and see what its relationship is to our daily life.

3

The Full Significance of Death

THE AVERAGE PERSON wastes his life. He has a great deal of energy but he wastes it. He spends his days in the office, or in digging the garden, or as a lawyer, or he leads the life of a sannyasin. The life of an average person seems, at the end, utterly meaningless, without significance. When he looks back, when he is fifty, eighty, or ninety, he asks what he has done with his life.

Life has a most extraordinary significance, with its great beauty, its great suffering and anxiety. At the end of it all, what have we done with life? Money, sex, the constant conflict of existence, the weariness, the travail, unhappiness, and frustrations are all we have, with perhaps occasional joy; or perhaps you love someone completely, wholly, without any sense of self.

There seems to be so little justice in the world. Philosophers have talked a great deal about justice. The social workers talk about justice. The average person wants justice. But is there justice in life at all? One is clever, well placed, with a good mind, and is good-looking, having everything he or she wants. Another has nothing. One is well educated, sophisticated, free to do what he or she wants. Another is a cripple, poor in mind and in heart. One is capable of writing and speaking, and is a good human being. Another is not. One is fair, another is dark. One is bright, aware, sensitive, full of feeling, loving a beautiful sunset, the glory of the moon, the astonishing light on the water; one sees all that, and another does not. One is reasonable, sane, healthy, and another is not.

So one asks, seriously, is there justice in the world at all? Can human beings ever have justice? When one looks around, life seems so empty and meaningless for most people. Before the law all are supposedly equal, but some are more equal than others who have not sufficient money to employ good lawyers. Some are born high, others low. This has been the problem of philosophy, the love of truth, love of life. But perhaps truth is in life, not in books, not in ideas, not separate from life. Perhaps truth is where we are and in how we live.

As we observe all this in the world, there is apparently very little justice. So where is justice then? It appears that there is justice only when there is compassion. Compassion is the ending of suffering. Compassion is not born out of any religion or from belonging to any cult. You cannot have your superstitions and invented gods and become compassionate. To have compassion there must be complete and total freedom from all conditioning. Is such freedom possible?

The human brain has been conditioned over millions of years. That is a fact. And it seems that the more knowledge we acquire about all the things of the earth and heavens, the more we get bogged down. When there is compassion, then with it there is intelligence, and that intelligence has the vision of justice. We have invented the ideas of karma and reincarnation, and we think that by inventing those ideas, those systems about something that is to happen in the future, we have solved the problem of justice. Justice begins only when the mind is very clear and when there is compassion.

Our brains are very complex instruments. Your brain, or my brain, is of the brain of humanity. It has not just developed from when we were born until now. It has evolved through endless time and conditions our consciousness. That consciousness is not personal, it is the ground on which all human beings stand. When you observe this consciousness with all its content of beliefs, dogmas, concepts, fears, pleasures, agonies, loneliness, depression, and despair, it is not your individual consciousness. It is not that the individual holds this consciousness. We are deeply conditioned to think that we are separate individuals, but it is not your brain or mine. We are not separate.

Our brains are so conditioned through education, through religion, to think we are separate entities with separate souls and so on. We are not individuals at all. We are the result of thousands of years of human experience, human endeavor and struggle.

So, we are conditioned; therefore we are never free. As long as we live with or by a concept, a conclusion, with certain ideas or ideals, our brains are not free and therefore there is no compassion. Where there is freedom from all conditioning, which is freedom from being a Hindu, a Christian, a Muslim, or a Buddhist, freedom from being caught up in specialization (though specialization has its place), freedom from giving one's life entirely to money, then there can be compassion.

As long as the brain is conditioned, as it is now, there is no freedom for humanity. There is no ascent through knowledge, as some philosophers and biologists are saying. Knowledge is necessary to drive a car, to do business, to go somewhere, to bring about technological development, and so on. But the psychological knowledge that one has gathered about oneself, which culminates in memory, is the result of external pressures and inward demands, and is not necessary.

Our lives are broken up, fragmented, divided. They are never whole; we never have holistic observation. We observe from a particular point of view. We are in ourselves broken up so that our lives are in contradiction in themselves; therefore there is constant conflict. We never look at life as a whole, complete and indivisible. The word *whole* means to be healthy, to be sane; it also means holy. That word has great significance. It is not that the various fragmented parts become integrated in our human consciousness. We are always trying to integrate various contradictions. But is it possible to look at life as a whole, to see the suffering, the pleasure, the pain, the tremendous anxiety, the loneliness, going to the office, having a house, sex, having children, as though they were not separate activities, but a holistic movement, a unitary action? Is that possible at all? Or must we everlastingly live in fragmentation and therefore be forever in conflict?

Is it possible to observe the fragmentation and the identification with those fragments? To observe, not correct, not transcend, not run away from or suppress, but observe. It is not a matter of what to do about it because, if you attempt to do something about it, you are then acting from a fragment and therefore cultivating further fragments and divisions. Whereas, if you can observe holistically the whole movement of life as one, then not only does conflict with its destructive energy cease, but also out of that observation comes a totally new approach to life.

I wonder if one is aware of how broken up one's daily life is? And if one is aware, does one then ask how to bring it all together to make a whole? And who is the entity, the "I," who is to bring all these various parts together and integrate them? Isn't that entity also a fragment? Thought itself is fragmentary, because knowledge is never complete about anything. Knowledge is accumulated memory, and thought is the response of that memory, and therefore it is limited. Thought can never bring about a holistic observation of life.

So, can one observe the many fragments that are our daily life and look at them as a whole? One is a professor, or a teacher, or a householder, or a sannyasin who has renounced the world; those are fragmented ways of living a daily life. Can one observe the whole movement of one's fragmented life with its separate and separative motives? Can one observe them all without the observer? The observer is the past, the accumulation of memories. The observer is that past and that is time. The past is looking at this fragmentation; and the past, as memory, is also in itself the result of previous fragmentations.

So, can one observe without time, without thought, without the remembrances of the past, and without the word? Because the word is the past, the word is not the thing. One is always looking through words, through explanations, which are movements of words. We never have a direct perception. Direct perception is insight that transforms the brain cells themselves. One's brain has been conditioned through time and functions in thinking. It is caught in that cycle. When there is pure observation of any problem, there is a transformation, a mutation, in the very structure of the cells.

We have created psychological time as hope, time as achievement. We are masters of that inward time that thought has put together. That is why we must understand the nature of time, which man has created. Why have human beings, psychologically, inwardly, created time—time when one will be good; time when one will be free of violence; time to achieve enlightenment; time to achieve some exalted state of mind; time as meditation? When one functions within the realm of that time, one is bringing about a contradiction and hence conflict. Psychological time is conflict.

It is really a great discovery if one realizes the truth that one is the past, the present, and the future, which is time as psychological knowledge. This creates a division in our consciousness between our living and the distant time that is death. That is, one is living with all one's problems, and death is something to be avoided, postponed, put at a great distance, that is another fragmentation in one's life. To observe holistically the whole movement of life is to live both the living and the dying. But one clings to life and avoids death; one does not even talk about it. So not only has one fragmented one's life, superficially, physically, but also one has separated oneself from death.

What is death? Is it not part of one's life? One may be frightened, one may want to avoid death and to prolong living, but always at the end of it there is death.

What is living? What is living, which is our consciousness? Consciousness is made up of its content; and the content is not different from consciousness. Consciousness is what one believes, one's superstitions, the gods, the rituals; one's greed, ambitions, competitiveness; the depth of one's loneliness, attachment, suffering. All that is one's consciousness, which is oneself. But that consciousness is not one's own; it is the consciousness of humanity. One is the world and the world is oneself. One is one's consciousness with its content.

That content is the ground upon which all humanity stands. Therefore, psychologically, inwardly, one is not an individual. Outwardly one may have a different form from another, be yellow, brown, black, tall or short, be a woman or a man, but inwardly, deeply, we are similar, perhaps with some variations, but the similarity is like a string that holds the pearls together.

We must comprehend what living is, then we can ask what dying is. What is before death is more important than what happens after death. Before the end, long before the last minute, what is living? Is living the travail and conflict without any relationship with each other? Is the sense of deep, inward loneliness what we call living? To escape from this so-called living, you go off to churches, temples, pray and worship, which is utterly meaningless. If you have money you indulge in extravagance. You know all the tricks you play to escape from your own consciousness, from your own state of mind. And this is what is called living.

Death is the ending of everything that you know. It is the ending of every attachment— all the money you have accumulated, which you cannot take with you—therefore you are frightened. Fear is part of your life. And so whatever you are, however rich, however poor, however highly placed, whatever power you have, there is the ending, which is called death.

And what is it that is dying? It is the "me" with all the accumulations that it has gathered in this life, all the pain, the loneliness, the despair, the tears, the laughter, the suffering that is the "me" with all its words. The summation of all this is "me." I may pretend that I have in me some higher spirit, the atman, the soul, something everlasting, but that is all put together by thought. And thought is not sacred.

So our life is this "me" that you cling to, to which you are attached. And the ending of that is death. It is the fear of the known, and the fear of the unknown. The known is our life, and we are afraid of that life; and the unknown is death, of which we are also afraid.

Death is the total denial of the past, present, and the future, which is "me." And being frightened of death, you think there are other lives to be lived. You believe in reincarnation; that is a nice, happy projection of comfort, invented by people who have not understood what living is. They see living is pain, constant conflict, endless misery with an occasional flare of smile, laughter, and joy, and they say, "We will live again next life; after death I will meet my wife or husband, my son, my god." Yet we have not understood what we are and what we are attached to. One has to inquire very closely and deeply into one's attachment. Death does not permit one to have anything when one dies.

Can the brain, the human consciousness, be free of this fear of death? As one is the master of psychological time, can one live with death and not keep it separate as something to be avoided, to be postponed, something to be put away? Death is part of life. Can one live with death and understand the meaning of ending? That is to understand the meaning of negation; ending one's attachments, ending one's beliefs, by negating. When one negates, ends, there is something totally new. So, while living, can one negate attachment completely? That is living with death.

Death is an ending and has extraordinary importance in life. Not suicide, not euthanasia, but the ending of one's attachments, one's pride, one's antagonism or hatred for another. When one looks holistically at life, then the dying, the living, the agony, the despair, the loneliness, and the suffering are all one movement. When one sees holistically, there is total freedom from death. There is a sense of ending and therefore there is no continuity; there is freedom from the fear of not being able to continue, even though the body will be destroyed.

When one human being understands the full significance of death, there is the vitality, the fullness, that lies behind that understanding; he is out of the human consciousness. Life and death are one when you begin to end in living; then you are living side by side with death. When you understand that, it is the most extraordinary thing to do. There is neither the past nor the present nor the future, there is only the ending.

4

Understand What Love Is

THOUGHT IS associated with other thoughts, it is a series of movements that we call thinking. One thought cannot exist by itself; there is not one thought without all the associations in connection with it. And thinking is the very life of us; that is so obvious. Thought is always in relation to something, and in pursuing one thought, other thoughts arise. I am polishing my shoes and look out of the window and see the mountains, and I am off! And I have to come back to polishing my shoes. I want to concentrate on something and the thought shoots off in another direction. I pull it back and try to concentrate. This goes on all the time from childhood until we die. And the more I think about thought, the more thought there is: "I shouldn't think along those lines, I must think rightly"; "Is there right thinking, is there wrong thinking, is there purposeful thinking?"; "What is the purpose of my life?"; and so on. The whole process of thinking begins and there is no end to it.

Thought has done the most extraordinary things. Technologically, it has done the most appalling things, terrifying things. It has built all the rituals of every religion, and it has tortured human beings. It has expelled people from one part of the world to another. Thought, whether Eastern or Western, is still thinking; it is not Eastern thinking and Western thinking, two separate things.

Is there an end to thought? Not to your way of thinking, or my way of thinking, and all of us thinking together, moving in the same direction. We are asking whether thought can ever stop. That is, is there an end to time? Thinking is the result of knowledge, memory. To acquire knowledge, one needs time. Even the computer, which is so extraordinary, has to be given a split second before it gallops out what it wants to say. So when we are asking whether thought can ever end, we are also asking whether there is a stop to time. It is a rather interesting question if you go into it.

What does time mean to us, not only psychologically but outwardly—sunset, sunrise, learning a language, and so on? You need time to go from here to there, even by the fastest train or airplane. As long as there is a distance between what is and what might be, what I am and what I will be, whether it is a very short distance or centuries of distance, that distance can only be covered in time. So time implies evolution. You plant the seed in the earth; it takes a whole season to mature, grow, or a thousand years to become a full tree. Everything that grows or becomes needs time. Everything. So time and thought are not two separate movements. They are one solid movement.

We are asking whether thought and time have an end, a stop. How will you find out? This has been one of the problems confronting the human being from the beginning. This movement of time is a circle; time is a bondage. Hope involves time. So man has asked not if there is timelessness but rather if there is an end to time.

This is really a very serious question. We are not inquiring into the timeless. We are asking whether time, which is thought, has a stop. Now, how will you discover that? Through analysis? Through so-called intuition? That word, *intuition,* which has been used so much, may be most dangerous. It may be our hidden desire; it may be our deeply rooted motive of which we are not aware; it may be the prompting of our tendency, our own idiosyncrasy, our own particular accumulation of knowledge. We are asking, if you put all that aside, has time a stop? How will you find out? *You,* not anybody else, because what others say has no importance.

We have to inquire very deeply into the nature of time just as we went very deeply into the nature of thinking. Can all that come to an end? Is it a gradual process? If it is a gradual process, the very gradualness is time, so the ending cannot be gradual; it cannot be "eventually." It cannot be next weekend or tomorrow, or a few minutes later. It cannot be the next second either. All that allows time. If one really grasps all this, deeply comprehends the nature of thought, the nature of time, discipline, the art of living—if one does not cover it up by all kinds of movements but stays with it quietly—then there is a glimpse of its nature, an insight into it that is not related to memory, to anything. Find out!

The speaker can easily say there is an ending. That would be too childish. Unless we actually investigate, experiment, push it, go into it deeply, we cannot come upon a strange sense of time-lessness.

How can our limited brain grasp the unlimited? It cannot, because it is limited. Can we grasp the significance, the depth, of the quality of the brain and recognize the fact—the fact, not the idea—that our brains are limited by knowledge, by specialities, by particular disciplines, by belonging to a group, a nationality? That is basically self-interest, camouflaged, hidden, by all kinds of things—robes, crowns, rituals. Essentially, this limitation comes into being when there is self-interest. That is so obvious. When I am concerned with my own happiness, with my own fulfilment, with my own success, that very self-interest limits the quality of the brain and the energy of the brain. That brain, for millions of years, has evolved in time, death, and thought. Evolution means a whole series of time events. To put all the religious rituals together needs time. So the brain has been conditioned, limited by its own volition, seeking its own security, keeping to its own backyard, saying, "I believe," "I don't believe," "I agree," "I don't agree," "This is my opinion," "This is my judgment." It is all self-interest, whether it is in the hierarchy of religion, or among the various noted politicians, or the person who seeks power through money, or the professor with his or her tremendous scholastic knowledge, or all the gurus who are talking about goodness, peace. It is all part of self-interest.

Our brain has become very small; we have reduced the quality of its immense capacity. Technologically, it has made tremendous improvements, and it also has immense capacity to go inwardly very, very deeply. But self-interest limits it. To discover for oneself where self-interest is hidden, is very subtle. It may hide behind an illusion, in neuroticism, in make-believe, in some family name. Uncover every stone, every blade of grass, to find out.

Either you take time to find out, which becomes a bondage, or you see the thing, grasp it, have an insight into it instantly. When you have a complete insight it covers the whole field.

How can the brain, which is conditioned, grasp the unlimited, which is beauty, love, and truth? What is the ground of compassion and intelligence, and can it come upon each one of us? Are you inviting compassion? Are you inviting intelligence? Are you inviting beauty, love, and truth?

Are you trying to grasp it? I am asking you. Are you trying to grasp the quality of intelligence, compassion, the immense sense of beauty, the perfume of love, and that truth that has no path to it? Is that what you are grasping, wanting to find out the ground upon which it dwells? Can the limited brain grasp this?

You cannot possibly grasp it, hold it, though you do all kinds of meditation, fast, torture yourself, become terribly austere, have only one piece of clothing. The rich cannot come to the truth, neither can the poor, nor the people who have taken a vow of celibacy, of silence, of austerity. All that is determined by thought, put together sequentially by thought; it is all the cultivation of deliberate thought, of deliberate intent. As the brain is limited, do whatever you will; sit cross-legged in the lotus posture, go off into a trance, meditate, stand on your head, or on one leg—

whatever you do, you will never come upon it; compassion does not come.

Therefore one must understand what love is. Love is not sensation. Love is not pleasure, desire, fulfillment. Love is not jealousy, hatred. Love has sympathy, generosity, and tact, but these qualities are not love. To understand that, to come to that, requires a great sense and appreciation of beauty. Not the beauty of a woman or of a man, or a cinema star. Beauty is not in the mountain, in the skies, in the valleys, or in the flowing river. Beauty exists only where there is love. And beauty, love, is compassion.

There is no ground for compassion; it does not stay at your convenience. That beauty, love, truth, is the highest form of intelligence. When there is that intelligence, there is action, clarity, a tremendous sense of dignity. It is something unimaginable. And that which is not to be imagined, or the unlimited, cannot be put into words. It can be described; philosophers have described it, but the philosophers who have described it are not that which they have described.

To come upon this great sense, there must be the absence of the "me," the ego, egocentric activity, the becoming. There must be a great silence in one. Silence means emptiness of everything. In that there is vast space. Where there is vast space there is immense energy—not self-interested energy, but unlimited energy.

Death is the most extraordinary thing, putting an end to long continuity. In that continuity we hope to find security, because the brain can only function excellently when it is completely secure—secure from terrorism, secure in a belief, secure in knowledge, and so on. All that comes to an end when there is death. I may have hope for a next life and all that stuff, but death is really the ending of a long continuity. I have identified myself with that continuity. That continuity is "me." And death says, "Sorry, old boy, that is the end." And you are not frightened of death, really not frightened, if you are living constantly with death, that is, constantly ending. Not continuing and ending, but ending every day that which you have gathered, that which you have memorized, that which you have experienced.

Time gives us hope, thought gives us comfort, thought assures us a continuity, and we say, "Well, in the next life . . ." But if I do not end this silliness now, the stupidity, the illusions, they

42

would be there in a next life, if there were a next life. Time, thought, give continuity, and we cling to that continuity, and therefore there is fear.

And fear destroys love. Love, compassion, and death are not separate movements.

Can we live with death, and can thought and time have a stop? They are all related. Do not separate time, thought, and death. It is all one thing.

5

Three Arts in Our Daily Life

I THINK WE ought to understand very clearly and simply the art of listening, the art of seeing, and the art of learning. The word *art* is generally applied to artists, those who paint, those who write poems, make sculpture, and so on. But the meaning of that word *art* is giving everything its right place, putting all our thoughts, feelings, anxieties, and so on, in their right place, giving the proper proportion to things, putting everything in harmony.

We rarely listen to anybody. We are so full of our own conclusions, our own experiences, our own problems, our own judgments, that we have no space in which to listen. To listen is possible only when you put aside your particular opinion, your particular knowledge or problem, your conclusions. Then you are free to listen without interpreting, judging, evaluating. Actually, the art of listening is to listen with great care, with attention, with affection. If you are capable of such listening, then communication becomes very simple. There will be no misunderstanding. Communication implies to think together, to share the things that we are talking about together, to partake in the problem as two human beings. Living in a monstrous, corrupt world where everything is so ugly, brutal, violent, and meaningless, communication seems very important to me. In the art of listening one learns immediately, one sees the fact instantly. In the art of listening there is freedom, and in that freedom every nuance of a word has significance and there is immediate comprehension. There is immediate insight and therefore immediate freedom to observe.

There is also the art of seeing, to see things as they are, not as you wish to see them; to see things without any illusion, without any preconceived judgment or opinion, to see what actually is, not your conclusions about what is.

Then, there is the art of learning. Not memorizing, which becomes very mechanical. Our brains have already become extraordinarily mechanical. The art of learning implies freedom to observe, to listen without prejudice, without argumentation, without any emotional, romantic responses.

If we actually, not intellectually, have these three arts in our daily life, putting everything in its right place, where it belongs, then we can live a really very quiet, harmonious life. So please learn now the art of listening. See with the attention of listening that thought is time, thought is measure, thought is a movement in time, which creates fear. If you do not make a conclusion of that statement, but actually listen with your heart, with your mind, with all your capacity, attention, and care, then you will see that fear has no place at all. The art of listening is the miracle.

So listen, not thinking what to do about it. The art of listening is to be sensitive, to be alert, to be watchful, *now*. If you are doing that now, you will see that you will put thought in its right place. Then you will have an actual relationship with another, and therefore never have conflict with another.

Our consciousness is our daily, everyday life. In that consciousness there is the desire for power, the many hurts that one has received from childhood. There is fear, pleasure, and the thing that we call *love,* which is not love. There are the innumerable beliefs that we have—belief in God or belief in no god, belief in socialism, belief in capitalism. Belief indicates a life that is based on make-believe, which has nothing to do with actuality.

We are bringing order in consciousness, not by wanting order, not by making an effort to bring about order, but by listening, seeing, learning. To listen there must be no direction. To see there must be no distortion. And to learn, not to memorize, there must be freedom to observe and to watch.

6

Laying the Foundation of Meditation

I WONDER OFTEN why we come together, listening to a speaker, half serious, curious, and not really wanting to change our life totally. We become rather mediocre, without a flair, without any quality of genius. I am using *genius* in the sense, not of any particular talent or particular gift, but of a mind that comprehends the totality of life, which is a vast, complex, contradictory, unhappy existence. One listens, and one goes away with partial understanding, with no deep intention and serious attention to bring about a deep psychological revolution. I wonder often why human beings tolerate the kind of lives they lead. You may blame the circumstances, the society, the political organization, but blaming others has not solved our problems. We drift and life seems such a waste, going to an office from morning till night for fifty years or so and then retiring to die or vegetate or grumble or fade away quietly.

When one looks at one's own life with all its extraordinary beauty, the vastness of what we have achieved technologically, one wonders why there has been so little beauty in our life. I mean by that word not merely the appearance of beauty, the decoration of the outer, but that quality of great communication with nature. If one loses contact with nature, one loses relationship with other human beings. You may read poems if you are so inclined, you may read all the beautiful sonnets and hear the lyrical swing of a lovely poem, but imagination is not beauty. The appreciation of a cloud and the love of light in that cloud, and of a sheet of water along a dry road, or a bird perched on a single branch—all that enchantment we rarely see or appreciate or love because we are occupied with our own problems, with our own worries, with our peculiar ideas and fixations, and are never free. Beauty is this quality of freedom that is totally different from independence.

When you hear all this, I wonder what you make of it. When we do not see a dog and love that dog, or a rock, or a stray cloud passing by, when we have not that sense of extraordinary communication with the world that brings about great beauty, we become small human beings, mediocre, wasting our extraordinary life and losing all the beauty and the depth of existence. We must get back to realities, but that is also real, extraordinarily real. The branch, the shadow, the light on a leaf, the fluttering parrot, is also actual, real, and when we understand the swaying palm tree and the whole feeling of life, then there is a great sense of depth to beauty. But I am afraid we are not interested in that. We listen, and let it slip by. It may sound romantic, sentimental, but beauty is not romantic, not sentimental, nor emotional. It is something very, very solid, like a rock in the midst of a fast-flowing stream.

We must investigate order, because our life is disorderly, confused, contradictory. We are talking very simply. Where there is contradiction, there is no order. Where there is confusion, conflict, there is no order; and our life, as we live it daily, is a mass of contradiction, confusion, conflict, and dishonesty. That is a fact. And one wonders if order can be brought about in this confusion, because without order there is no efficiency. Order has nothing whatever to do with sentiment, with romance. Order is sequential, logical, sane.

So, can we have order—not a blueprint, not something laid down by tradition or by a guru or by a leader or by our own little desires and compulsions—but lasting order? How can we bring about order in our lives so that there is no opposite, duality, contradiction, dishonesty, whether politically, religiously, or in our relationship with each other? We can go often into some kind of illusion and think that we are meditating, but without bringing about order in our daily life, do what we will, there can be no meditation. So we are laying the foundation of meditation.

The first thing is to realize how disorderly our daily life is, to be aware. It is not how to bring order in disorder, but to understand the nature of disorder. When I understand the nature of disorder, then out of that comprehension, out of that obvious fact, comes the beauty of order that is not imposed or disciplined or suppressed or from conformity. Out of the very investigating of disorder, order comes naturally. Now, let's do it.

Human beings have extraordinary capacity. Technologically, immense things have been done. Human beings are extraordinarily capable, have thought out almost every form of concepts, principles, ideas, religious projections; they have invented rituals, some of which are really most beautiful, but they have no meaning at all. The human mind has great qualities. The mind is not only the various forms of sensory activities, but is the emotions, affection, care, attention, the intellectual capacity, and that sense of great love. All that is the mind, the wholeness of the mind. Will you challenge that as we are talking, so that it shall operate at its highest, greatest excellence? Because if you do not challenge it, you live in disorder.

We are asking why human beings, for centuries upon centuries, have accepted living in disorder, politically, religiously, economically, socially, and in our relationship with each other. Why? Why have we accepted living this way?

From whom do you expect the answer? A challenge implies that you respond with your highest capacity. I have challenged your mind. The speaker has said: exercise your highest capacity, exercise all your energy to find out whether it is possible to live in a world that is degenerating, corrupt, immoral, whether you can live a sane life that is completely whole. That is your challenge. What is your response to it? The word *whole* means healthy, both physically and psychologically, with all the capacities of your mind; that is sanity. And the word *whole* also means holy, sacred. That is the whole of life.

Are you as a human being aware of the total disorder and the degenerating process going on in the world around you and in yourself? Aware in the sense of observing what is actually taking place. Not imagining what is taking place, not making an idea of what is taking place, but the actual happening: the political, the religious, the social, the moral degeneration of man. No institution, no guru, no higher principles, are going to stop this degradation. It is happening the world over. Are we aware of that? If we are, then what shall we do? What is our action? Not at some future date—what is our *immediate* action? Will we escape from the actual fact of the brain that is getting old, degenerating, or will we, together, investigate, explore, why human beings have become like this?

What shall we do? I would suggest that we first look at our life, at what it actually is, at what is happening in our life, because our life in action is society. Our life in action is our society, and you cannot transform that society unless you transform yourself. That is so obvious. The communist, the liberal, the socialist will not alter it. Reading the Gita or the Upanishads will not alter it, or becoming terribly interested in what Buddhism has to say, or following Zen meditation. None of those will solve it. So let us look at what is happening in our life, our daily life.

Our daily life is based on relationship. Without relationship you cannot possibly exist. What is your relationship with others, with your wife, with your husband, with your boss, with your factory worker, with your neighbor? What is the relationship with each other? In that relationship, is there order, or self-centered activity opposed to another self-centered activity?

That is contradiction. I may be married, have children, sex, and all the rest of it, and if I am self-centered, concerned about my own success, my ambition, my status, worrying about myself, and my wife is also concerned about herself, her problems, her beauty, her looks, how can there be any kind of relationship between the two people? If you have one belief and another has another kind of belief or another kind of conclusion, another kind of dogma, there is no relationship. Haven't you noticed all this? So, is it possible to bring order in your relationship, with your wife and husband, not with the universe, not with cosmos, not with "God"? God is an invention of the intellect. You can have extraordinary relationship with those things that you have invented, deal with illusions, but to have relationship with your wife and husband and children so that there is no conflict, that is where order begins.

Now, how will you bring order there? Order is sequence in space—listen to the beauty of it. Space in the mind. That means a mind that is never occupied with any problem. But our minds are so occupied, so crowded with belief, with pursuit of all kinds of things, confusion, illusion, that there is no space. Where there is no space, there cannot be sequence and order. And if there is no order in our daily life, meditation is merely an escape from your life. And escape into meditation leads only to illusion.

So one must lay the foundation to find out that which is beyond thought, that which is immeasurable, that which has no word. But that cannot come into being without this sense of great order in which there is total freedom.

7

The Art of Living

MOST OF US are fragmented, broken up into business life, religious life, family life, sexual life, and so on. We are not holistic, whole human beings. We look at life from a particular point of view, from a conclusion, or from some idealistic concept. These are all a fragmented outlook on life. Can we face a problem from a wholly different outlook that is not fragmented at all? Recognizing, being aware that we are fragmented, broken up, divided in ourselves, contradictory, opposing one desire against another desire, is it possible that we could face a problem from a different focus?

Why do we have problems? We have multiple problems in life, and problems are increasing in a society that is so sophisticated, so complex, overpopulated, with bad governments, and so on. In the resolution of one problem we seem to increase many other problems. Why do we have problems, and is it possible to meet a problem without a brain that is already conditioned to solve problems?

Let's look at it. We go to school very young, age five or seven, and as children we are faced with problems: how to write, how to read, how to learn mathematics. So from childhood our brain is conditioned to solving problems. One goes to college where there are again problems; then university, jobs, various functions, vocations, and so on, problem after problem. Our brain is full of problems. And we are always seeking solutions from a brain that is conditioned to solve problems. Now, how can the brain solve problems if it is not free from problems?

Our brains are conditioned from childhood to the resolution of problems. Because the brain is conditioned to solve problems, it is always seeking a solution. It is not understanding the problem itself but seeking the solution of the problem.

Is it possible to have a brain that is not conditioned to problems?

Our brain is conditioned now to the solution of problems, and we have never solved the problems. They are increasing more and more. Why? Is it because a conditioned brain, which is embedded in problems, can never solve problems? Is it possible to have a brain that is not conditioned to the solution of problems and so can understand problems? Isn't there a difference between the solving of a problem and the understanding of a problem? In the understanding of a problem, the solution may lie in the problem.

Take a very ordinary example. We have never stopped wars. Human beings have had wars since they came on this earth. We have never solved the problem of war. We decided to reorganize how to kill man better—and this is called progress. This is not a joke. We move from organization to organization. First we had the League of Nations, and now we have the United Nations, but wars go on. We move from one organization to another, hoping thereby to solve problems. And we multiply problems and never stop wars.

The cause of wars is nationalism, economic division, local division. Linguistic, racial, religious, economic, and cultural divisions divide us. We are all human beings, we all suffer, we all have pain and anxiety, boredom, loneliness, despair. We do not tackle that, but we want to solve the problems that seem to have external causes.

Can the brain, recognizing, seeing that it is conditioned to the solution of problems from childhood, be free of the conditioning and then face problems? Will you do it? That is the question. Can we be conscious, be aware that our brain, that we as human beings, from the beginning of life, are always struggling with problems and trying to find the right answer to them? The right answer can be only when we recognize that the brain is conditioned and that as long as that brain is conditioned to solving problems we will never find the right answer.

If one cannot get on with one's wife, one divorces, then chooses another person, and keeps on repeating this. If one has plenty of time and energy this is the game that is going on in the world, on a smaller or bigger scale. But the problem is not divorce and all the complications of relationship, but to understand the depth of relationship, the meaning of relationship. Relationship, as we pointed out, is one of the most important things in life; not the emotional expressions of it, the tantrums, the neuroticism of relationship, but depth in relationship. And we never ask about that. We want to solve the problem of relationship—and so we never solve it. The psychiatrists, psychotherapists, and so on, are multiplying in the world like mushrooms. And they are not solving problems. They are not solving the depth of all this.

We should consider together the art of living. What is the art of living? We have the art of poetry, painting, the art of cooking, and so on. But we have never asked ourselves what the art of living is, which is, perhaps, the greatest art. Is there an art, or is it all just chance, some genetic, biological chance? If you make a problem of it, then the art is thrown out of the window.

So, let's look together to find out what the art of living is, using *art* with the width and the depth of that word, not just as the contents of a museum. If you were asked what the art of living is, what would your answer be? A calculated answer, personal answer, or emotional or romantic answer is meaningless. Right? If I answer that question emotionally—oh, the art of living is the highest aspiration, or the art of living is the most exalted intellectual activity—it is sheer nonsense; that is only very partial. Or to say that the art of living is to have a holistic outlook on life—it sounds excellent but factually it is not. So what is the art of living? Obviously, it is to have no conflict whatsoever. A brain that is in conflict all the time, that has problems all the time, tremendous self-concern, such a brain must inevitably be limited. If one is thinking about oneself, for example, how to meditate or whether you can, your very meditation is self-centeredness. You can add more to it, but it appears that the art of living is to live without conflict.

Is that possible at all? That is, to understand the opposing elements in one's life, desiring one thing, and opposing that with another desire. You know this corridor of dualities. As long as self-centeredness exists, there must be conflict, because self-centeredness is limited, small, petty. You hear all this but you carry on. You say that it is not possible in modern society to live without self-centeredness—at least a little bit of it. Have you ever tried? Have you ever lived without self-centeredness for one day, not thinking about yourself? Even just for an hour! And see what happens. You haven't committed to anything! You can go back to your self-centeredness, nobody is going to say how wrong it is, or how right it is; that is the normal state of human beings, apparently. So, really try for an hour actually to do it—not try it, do it—and see what happens. And if you do it for one hour you can extend it. And it gives you tremendous energy. It gives you a great sense of passion, not lust and all that, but passion to pursue something profoundly to the very end.

What is attention? Is it a physical act? Is it the movement of thought? Is it an action of desire, which is the essence of will? How does attention come about? Can it come naturally, easily, without making tremendous effort, without going to college, or attending some guru, being trained? We are going to look at the question, not the answer.

Attention implies not only the hearing of the ear but hearing without the ear. Attention also implies seeing, perceiving; seeing visually, but also seeing with the inner eye, as it were. Attention also means learning. Seeing, hearing, and learning. Those three things are implied.

What is learning? Is it memorizing as we do when we go to school, college, university, memorizing, storing up knowledge from books, from professors, from teachers, from housemasters, and so on and so on? That is always accumulating knowledge and using that knowledge, skillfully or not. An apprentice to a master carpenter is learning the nature of the wood, the kinds of wood, the grain, the beauty of the wood, the feeling of the wood, and the instruments that he is employing. He is learning; and that learning is through experience, day after day, month after month, accumulating knowledge about carpentry. That is what we call learning. That kind of learning is limited, obviously, because all knowledge is limited, now or in the past or in the future.

Is there a learning that is not limited? Is there a learning that is not an accumulative process of learning knowledge, but in which is implied hearing not only the words, the significance of the words, your reactions to the words, your responses to certain favorite words, like *love* and *hate,* but also seeing without any prejudice, seeing without the word? Can you look at a tree without the word? Have you ever done this? That means seeing without direction, without motive, without any network of thought blocking the seeing. Learning is a limitless process.

Attention implies all that. And the beginning of it is to be aware. Are we aware of our surroundings as we sit here, looking at it all without a single word? To be aware. But in awareness you begin to choose—I like that blue shirt better than what I am wearing. I like the way your hair is done, better than mine. You are always comparing, judging, evaluating, which is choice. Can we be aware without choice?

Will you do it? If we are doing this, then we begin to discover that awareness is entirely different from concentration. Concentration implies focusing all thought on a particular subject, on a particular page, on a particular word. Which implies cutting off all other thoughts, building resistance to every other thought, which then becomes narrow, limited. So concentration is limited. But you have to concentrate when you are doing something. When you are washing dishes, you have to wash them very carefully, use the right kind of soap, the right kind of water. You know all this. Awareness without choice, which means without concentration, is to be aware without judging, evaluating, condemning, comparing, and from that, move. That is attention, which is natural.

When I want to listen to a story you are telling me, a very exciting thriller, I listen to you very carefully. When you are telling me something very, very serious, I am so eager, so attentive to understand what you are saying that I pay attention. I understand what I am thinking about, that is irrelevant, but I am tremendously concerned with what you are saying. Therefore I am all attention; all my nerves, my whole being, wants to understand what you are talking about.

In that attention there is no "me." Get it? When there is this tremendous attention, which means when all my energy is given to understand, I am not thinking about myself. Therefore there is no center in me that says "I must attend."

8

Be Completely Free of Fear

I AM GOING TO investigate something totally new, and I hope you will have the kindness and the seriousness to listen, not agreeing or disagreeing but thinking together logically, sanely, rationally, and with a certain sense of humility.

Skill becomes all important in life, because that is the means of earning a livelihood. Our universities, colleges, and schools are directed for that purpose. When one is totally educated for that purpose, that skill invariably breeds a certain sense of power, arrogance, and self-importance. What is the relationship of skill to clarity?

And what is the relationship of clarity to compassion?

We have talked very often about the art of listening, the art of seeing, the art of learning. The art of listening is to listen so that naturally everything is put in its right place. The meaning of that word, *art,* is to put things where they belong. And the art of seeing is to observe without any distortion. Obviously. If there is any distortion there is no observation. To see clearly, to have great clarity in perception, there must be no distortion. Distortion is brought about by any form of motive, purpose, direction.

The art of learning is not only the accumulation of knowledge, which is necessary for skillful action, but also learning without accumulation. There are two types of learning. There is acquiring and gathering knowledge through experience, through books, through education; the brain is registering, accumulating knowledge, storing it up, and acts from that storage of knowledge, skillfully or unskillfully. Another form of learning is never to accumulate, is to become so totally aware that you only register what is absolutely necessary and nothing else. Then the mind is not cluttered up all the time with the movement of knowledge.

So, there are three essential things in the awakening of intelligence. There is the art of listening without distortion, and to communicate not only verbally but nonverbally exactly what you mean. The art of seeing is to observe clearly without a direction, without motive, without any form of desire, merely to observe. And the art of learning, accumulating knowledge, means registering all the things that are necessary for skillful action, and not registering any psychological responses, any psychological reactions, so that the brain is employing itself only where function and skill are necessary.

It is very arduous to be so totally aware that you register only what is necessary and absolutely do not register anything that is not necessary. Someone insults you, someone flatters you, someone calls you this or that, and there is no registration. It gives tremendous clarity to register what is necessary and not to register what is not necessary, so there is no psychological building up of the "me," the structure of the self. The structure of the self arises only when there is registration of everything that is not necessary. That is, giving importance to one's name, form, one's experience, one's opinions, conclusions; all that is the gathering up of the energy of the self, which is always distorting.

Listening without any conclusion, without any opinion, which are distorting factors, one discovers the false and the true without any effort, because when there is actual attention given to listening, that very attention excludes everything that is not absolutely factual. When you observe with conclusions, opinions, dogmas, beliefs, you cannot possibly see very clearly. Learning to act skillfully in life is necessary, but any other form of registering distorts, gives importance to skill and therefore becomes mechanical.

The art of listening, the art of seeing, the art of learning give extraordinary clarity, and that clarity can communicate verbally. If there is no clarity, skill in action breeds self-importance, whether that self-importance is identified with a group or with oneself, or with a nation. And that self-importance denies clarity, naturally. You cannot have clarity without compassion. Because we have no compassion, skill has become more important.

Clarity is denied when there is any form of fear. Most human beings have a great deal of fear—which denies compassion.

Fear in any form, both physiological as well as psychological, distorts clarity; therefore, a person who is afraid in any way has no compassion. There are various forms of fear—of growing old, of losing your husband, wife, child, fear of not being successful. You do not have to invite fear; it is there. So you can look at the fear now, because you are a living human being now and in that state your fears, though they may be dormant, are still there consciously or unconsciously.

The art of seeing, the art of observing very clearly, is possible only when you do not want to get rid of fear, because then that becomes a distorting factor. If you are unconscious of your fears, that is also a distorting factor. The many fears have a common root. It is like a tree that has many branches and leaves. Fear also has many branches, many leaves, many expressions of fear that breed their own flowering and their own fruit, which is action. So one must go to the very root of fear, not take various forms of fears but the root of fear.

Look: one may be afraid of darkness, one may

be afraid of losing one's wife or husband, one may be afraid of having no money, one may be afraid of some past pain and not want it again, one may be afraid of a dozen things. One can go through them analytically one by one—and that is such a waste of time, isn't it? Whereas it would be much simpler and more direct if you go to the root of fear.

I think many of us do not realize or are aware deeply of the nature of fear and what it does to human beings. When there is fear, there are many kinds of neurotic action. Most of you are lonely, and so you seek companionship, escaping from loneliness. Companionship becomes very important, and if you have no companionship fear arises. Or out of that loneliness you build a wall around yourself; you resist, you escape, and out of that escape, resistance, suppression, grows every form of neurotic action. So it is very important to understand the nature and the structure of fear, because it will not give clarity. And if there is no clarity there is no awakening of intelligence, which is neither yours nor mine. That intelligence has its own action, which is non-mechanistic, and therefore without cause.

So it is very important to understand fear and be completely free of it. Do we see the importance and the urgency of wiping fear away, conscious fear and fears of which we are not conscious? One can deal with conscious fears comparatively easily, but it is much more difficult to be free of fears of which you do not know, fears that are hidden. How are you going to examine the deep-rooted fears? Is it possible to examine them? Psychologists say it is possible through analysis, through dreams, through careful psychoanalytical therapy. Analysis does not clear up the mind. There is no clarity in analysis because the more you analyze, the more there is to analyze. And it might take you the whole of your life; at the end of it you have nothing!

We are going to think together to find out the truth of analysis, the *truth*, not yours or mine. First of all, in analysis there is the observer and the observed, the analyzer and the analyzed. The analyzer says, "I am going to analyze my reactions, my dreams, my desires, my fears." But is the analyzer different from the fear, different from what he is going to analyze? You must be very clear on this. Is the analyzer different from the analyzed? If you say they are different, which most people do, then you are caught in everlasting conflict. That is, when the analyzer examines his responses—jealousy, anger, violence—in that examination, in that analysis, the examiner thinks he is separate. And this separation will inevitably divide, and therefore there must be conflict. Where there is division, there must be conflict, whether the division is between two nations or between man and woman. Not that the woman is the same as the man; obviously, biologically they are not. But the ideas, the accumulated responses of each, the images they have of each other, divide, and therefore there is conflict in relationships.

So, when there is analysis, there must inevitably be conflict. Most unfortunately, we are educated to have conflict. It is the way of our life; if we have no conflict we say, "What is wrong with me?" And to have conflict is the essence of neuroticism.

And in analysis time is necessary. It might take days, months, years; if you have the energy, the capacity, the money, then you can go on analyzing yourself endlessly. It becomes quite fun! Then you have somebody to go to, to tell them all about your troubles and pay whatever you pay. That is such a waste of time. It is postponement of the immediate solution of the problem. Analysis implies conflict, analysis implies time, analysis implies no ending to any problem. That is a fact. So when you see the truth of this, or see the fact, you will never analyze.

Then what will you do? Psychologically, analysis not only breeds time, division, but also each analysis must be complete, mustn't it? Otherwise the incompleteness of analysis is brought over from yesterday, and with the incomplete analysis you examine the new fact. So there is always a coloring of the present from the past. If you see this very clearly, and I hope you do, then what will you do if you do not analyze? If you see analysis is a false process, if you yourself actually see the truth that analysis does not lead anywhere, then what will you do?

Now we are going to take fear. Most of us are accustomed to analyze fear, its cause and the effect. What has made one afraid? One seeks the cause. That is a process of analysis. It may be a hundred causes, or it may be a single cause. And the effect becomes the cause for the next fear. So there is causation, effect, and the effect becomes the cause. So when you are seeking a cause you are caught up in this chain, and therefore there is no release from this chain. This is part of analysis.

So one asks, "If there is no analysis, then what will happen to my fear?" There may be a dozen fears but we are concerned with the root, not with the branches. If you can pull out the root it is finished, the whole tree is dead. So, what is the root of fear? Is it time? One form of time is chronological, time by the watch, twenty-four hours, sunset to sunrise. There is another form of time that is psychological time. That is the "tomorrow." Psychologically, I will solve my problems the day after tomorrow. So is fear the result of time? I have had pain yesterday or last week, and that pain is registered in the brain. And when that pain is registered, then there is fear of that pain happening again a week later. When there is no registration of the pain, then there is no fear.

There is fear when there is measurement. When one measures oneself against somebody else, there is fear. I am not as intelligent as you are, and I would like to be as intelligent as you are, and I am afraid I may not be. All that is a movement of time, which is measurement, which is comparison. So measurement, time, comparison, imitation breed fear. And that time, measurement, comparison, is the movement of thought. So thought is the very root of fear. Please see the logic, the reasoning of this.

We are thinking together, examining together, taking the journey together to find out. And we see analysis is not the solution; finding the cause is not the solution; and time is not the solution, time being measurement, comparison. Time is the movement of thought. So the problem then is not how to be free of fear, or how to suppress fear, but to understand the whole movement of thought. See how far we have gone away from the demand to be free of fear? We are entering into something much greater, much more comprehensive. If there is understanding of the whole movement of thought, it must be holistic, whole. And fear arises only when there is the "me," which is the small, not the whole.

In the art of learning, the art of seeing, the art of listening, there is no movement of thought. If I am just listening to you, why should I interfere with my thoughts? I am seeing, observing; in that observation there is no movement of thought. I just observe. I observe the mountain, the tree, the river, the people, without any projection of my background and so on, which is the movement of thought. Thought is necessary to accumulate knowledge to function skillfully, but otherwise thought has no place whatsoever. And this brings tremendous clarity, doesn't it?

I hope you have clarity. Clarity means there is no center from which you are functioning, no center put together by thought as the "me," "mine," "they" and "we." Where there is a center, there must be a circumference, and where there is a circumference, there is resistance, there is division, and that is one of the fundamental "causes" of fear—*causes* in quotes.

So when we consider fear, we are considering the whole movement of thought, which breeds fear. And clarity is possible only when thought is completely in abeyance; that is, when thought has its right place, which is to act in the field of knowledge and not enter into any other field. In that, there is total elimination of all opinion, judgment, evaluation. There is only listening, seeing, and learning. Without clarity, skill becomes a most destructive thing in life, which is what is happening in the world. You can go to the moon and put the flag of your country up there, which is not clarity. You can kill each other through wars, by the extraordinary development of technology, which is the movement of thought. You can divide yourselves into races, communes, and so on and so on, which are all divisions created by thought.

Thought is a fragment. Thought is limited. Thought is conditioned. Thought is narrow, because thought is based on experience, memory, knowledge, which is the past, which is time-binding. That which is time-binding is necessarily limited, therefore thought is limited. So thought can never understand that which is whole. Thought can never understand that which is immeasurable, which is timeless. One can imagine the timeless, the immeasurable; thought can put up all kinds of imaginary future structures. But it is still limited. So, "God" put together by thought is limited. I am afraid those of you who believe in God won't see this, because your God is the result of your thought, of your fears, of your desire to be secure.

Please see the truth of this, and clarity will come like sun out of the clouds. See that thought is the word, and that the word is never the thing.

The word is the description of the thing, but the thing is not the description. Fear then becomes completely useless, it has no meaning. Then you have to find out whether thought can ever remain in its field and not move out of that field to register.

It is the function of the brain to register so that it can be secure, so that it can be safe. It is safe, secure in the field of knowledge. You cannot live without security. One must have food, clothing, and shelter, not for the few but for the whole. And that is only possible when thought only operates in that field and when it does not register in any other direction. Then there is no nationality, there is no "you" and "me." There is no division, because when there is no registration the mind is free to look, the mind is free to observe.

When there is that clarity, skill never becomes mechanical, because whatever the skill may be, it is functioning, acting from that clarity that is born out of compassion. One has to inquire very deeply into what compassion is. We have talked very clearly about clarity and skill, and the dangers of skill without clarity. There are three things, which are compassion, clarity, and skill.

And when there is compassion, there is no division between clarity and skill, it is one movement. Because we are caught up in skill, we do not see the total movement.

What is the nature and the structure of compassion? To understand it, one must go into pleasure, love, suffering, death. You cannot just say, "I have compassion." The mind that says "I am compassionate" is not compassionate. When the mind says, "I am intelligent," it is no longer intelligent because it is conscious of itself; when it is conscious of itself there is no intelligence.

To go into the depth and the meaning and the significance and the beauty of compassion, we must inquire not only, as we did, into fear, but also into pleasure. Is love pleasure? Is love desire? Is love of another a remembrance? Is love of another an image? All these are involved when we think over together this matter of compassion. And we can go into it only when we go together. Because a human being is not alone, one human being is the essence of all human beings. That is a fact; that is a reality. It is not my invention, my wanting to identify myself with the whole.

The absolute fact is that you, as a human being, living through millennia after millennia, are the representative of the whole of humanity that has suffered, agonized, shed tears, killed and been killed, that is jealous, angry, anxious, seeking pleasure, caught in fear. You are all that. Therefore you are the entire humanity. And when there is a total revolution in this consciousness, that revolution affects the consciousness of humanity. That is a fact. And that is why it is so urgently important that each one of us listens, is good enough to listen, is serious enough to take the journey together. When you fundamentally, deeply do that, when consciousness changes its content, you affect the whole of humanity.

9

All the Senses Highly Awakened

WHAT IS BEAUTY? Is beauty according to a principle, according to certain rules? Or, though there must be attention to proportion and so on, is beauty something entirely different? When you see mountains, range after range, blue in the evening, and when the sun touches them in early morning before everything else, the reaction to that seeing is great silence. You keep quiet; there is space, enormous space, between you and that—and beyond. When you see such marvelous beautiful mountains, snow-clad against the blue sky, for an instant you become silent. The very beauty, the very grandeur, the majesty of the mountains keeps you, makes you absolutely quiet. You can say, the shock of beauty. When you see something extraordinarily grand, of great height and depth, then the very shock of that beauty drives away for the moment all your problems. There is no self wondering, worrying, talking to itself; there is no entity, the self, the "me," looking. At that moment when the self is not, there is great beauty.

What is the role of art in our lives? Why should anything play a role in our lives? The greatest art is the art of living, not the paintings, the sculpture, the poems, and the marvelous literature. They have their place, but to find out for oneself the art of living is the greatest art. It surpasses any role in life.

Aesthetics is the capacity of perception, the capacity to perceive, which means one must be extraordinarily sensitive; and sensitivity comes from the depth of silence. It is no good going to colleges and universities to learn how to be sensitive, or to go to somebody to teach you how to be sensitive. You cannot perceive if there is not a certain depth of silence. If you look at trees in silence, there is a communication that is not merely verbal, but a communication, a communion with nature. Most of us have lost our relationship with nature: with the trees, with the mountain, with all the living things of the earth.

Sensitivity in our relationship is to be aware of each other. Is that at all possible? The art of living is to find a relationship that is not conflict, that is a flow of a harmonious manner of living together without all the quarrels, possessiveness and being possessed, and fear of loneliness—the whole cycle of human struggle. The art of living is far more important than the art of great painters. Listening to music, going into all the museums of the world and talking about them endlessly, reading books on art, all that may be an escape from our own troubles, anxieties, depressions.

Can we live an aesthetic life of deep perception, be aware of our words, be aware of noise, of the vulgarity of human beings? One learns far more in silence than in noise. These may sound like platitudes, but they are not. This requires a great deal of observation of oneself. That observation is prevented by any form of authority, looking to another to teach us how to observe. Just observe, watch the way we walk, the way we talk, the noise that goes on. Then out of that comes the art of living.

Art, as we said, is putting things together harmoniously. It is to observe the contradictions in oneself, one's desires that are always so strong, to observe all that, not create an opposite of it, just to observe the fact and live with the fact. It seems that is the way to bring about a life of harmony.

I hope you look at mountains, not at me. The speaker is not important at all. What he says may be important or may not be important, but you have to discover for yourself.

What is important in life? What is the root or the basic essential in life? As one observes more and more in television, and literature, magazines, and all the things that are going on, answers are becoming more and more superficial, quick. If you are in trouble, you go to specialists, and they tell you what to do. It is all becoming so superficial and vulgar—if one may use that word without any sense of being derogatory or insulting. It is all becoming rather childish.

One never asks what the fundamental questions are or what the fundamental necessity is for the depth of life. Surely it is not beliefs, dogmas, faith, not all the intellectual rigmarole, whether in the communist ideology or the Catholic theology, Marx or Lenin, or Saint Thomas Aquinas. They are all the same: theories, conclusions, and ideologies, based on belief, faith, dogma, rituals. So all that is becoming more and more superficial outwardly in one's life. And we live like that. This is a fact, I am not saying anything that is not so.

We have the marvelous worlds of entertainment, religion, and football—anything to escape. Yell, shout, never a quiet conversation, never looking at anything quietly, beautifully. So what is the fundamental, basic demand or basic thing that is really of the utmost importance in one's life?

Can thought be aware of itself? Thought has created the thinker separate from his thought. There is the thinker who says, "I must be aware of what I think, I must control my thoughts, I must not let my thoughts wander." And the thinker acts upon the thought. Now, is the thinker different from thought? Or has the thinking, thought, created the thinker? There is no thinker without thought.

Please, it is rather important to find out why this duality exists in us, the opposites, the contradiction: the "me" and the thought, the "me" as the thinker, the one who witnesses, the one who observes, and the thing to be observed. That is, the thinker then controls thought, shapes thought, puts thought into a mold. But is the thinker different from thought? Has not thought created the thinker?

Let us be logical. Verbally, intellectually, I can see very clearly that there is the division between the thinker and the thought, and that thought has created the thinker. So the thinker is the past, with his memories, with his knowledge, all put together by thought, which has come into being after experiences. So the thinker is the whole activity of the past. And then it says, "Thinking is something different from me, the thinker." We accept that logically, intellectually, very quickly. But why? Why do we say that we understand it intellectually? Why is the first re-action to say, "I understand intellectually"? Is it not because we never look at the whole thing? We only look at something intellectually. Why does one do that? Is it that the intellect is highly developed with most of us, or developed much more than our sensitivity, our immediate perception? Of course. Because we are trained from childhood to acquire, to memorize, to exercise certain parts of the brain to hold what it has been told, and keep on repeating it. So when we meet something new, we say, "I understand intellectually." We never meet the new totally, wholly, that is, with all our senses awakened. We never receive it completely; we receive it partially, and the partial activity is the intellectual activity. It is never the whole being observing. We say, "Yes, that is logical," and we stop there. We do not ask why it is that only part of the senses are awakened.

Intellectual perception is partial sensitivity, partial senses acting. In creating a computer you think intellectually, you do not have to have all your emotions and your senses. You have become mechanical, and repeat that. The same process is carried over when we hear something new. We understand intellectually, we do not meet it entirely. A statement is made but we do not receive it totally.

Why is it that we never meet anything—especially when we see a tree or the mountains, or the movement of the sea—with all our senses highly awakened? Isn't it that we live always partially, that we live in a limited sphere, a limited space in ourselves? It is a fact.

So to look, look with all your senses. When that takes place, when you look with all your senses, your eyes, your ears, your nerves, the whole response of the organism, which is also the brain, there is no center as the "me" who is looking.

We are asking if thought can be aware of itself. That is rather a complex question, and requires very careful observation. Thought has created wars through nationalism, through sectarian religions. Thought has created all this; God has not created the hierarchy of the church—the pope, all the robes, all the rituals, the swinging of the incense, the candles. All that paraphernalia that goes on in a cathedral or in a church is put together by thought, copied, some of it, from the ancient Egyptians, from the ancient Hindus, and Hebrews. It is all thought. So "God" is created by thought.

Does a person who has no fear whatsoever of dying or of living, who is without problems, need "God"? One can see what thought has done, step by step. So thought *can* be aware of its own action, so that there is no contradiction between the thinker and the thought, between the observer and the observed. When there is no contradiction, there is no effort. It is only when there is contradiction, which is division, that there must be effort.

So to find out whether it is possible to live a life without a single shadow of effort, contradiction, one must investigate the whole movement of thought. And one has not the time or the inclination; one is too busy, has too much to do. But one has plenty of time when one wants to play golf.

To find out the activity of thought, to watch it, is part of meditation.

Have you ever inquired into what silence is? What is silence? What is peace? Is peace between two wars? That is what is happening. What we call peace is between two wars. This war, like the next war, is to end all wars. Is peace between two noises? Is peace between two wars? Is peace between two quarrels?

So what is silence? It cannot be bought in a shop or pharmacy. We would like to buy it quickly and get on with it. But silence or peace cannot be bought. If that is so, what is silence?

Silence must mean space, mustn't it? I can be

very silent in a small space, enclose myself, shut my eyes, and put a wall round myself, concentrate on some petty little affair, and in that there can be a certain amount of peace, a certain amount of silence. I can go into my den, my reading room, or quiet room, and sit there; but the space is limited when I do that. Not only my little room, but in my brain also, the space is very, very limited. Because most of us have never even asked about, thought about all this.

So what is space? Is space from one point to another? Is space a limited dimension? Or is space without a center, and therefore without a border? As long as I have "me," my problems, my selfish demands, my, my, my, it is very limited. That limitation has its own small space. But that little space is a form of self-protective wall to remain within, not to be disturbed, not to have problems, not to have trouble, and so on. For most of us, that space of the self is the only space we have. And from that space we are asking what space is.

Where there is limitation, there cannot be vast space. That is all. And space implies silence. Noise does not imply space. With all the noise that is going on in towns, between people, and all the noise of modern music, there is no space. There is not silence anywhere, just noise. It may be pleasant or unpleasant, that is not the point.

So what does it mean to have space? The space between two notes on the piano is a very small space. Silence between two people who have been quarreling, and later on resume the quarreling, is a very limited space.

Is there a space that is limitless? Not in heaven, not in the universe, but in ourselves, in our whole way of living? To have space—not imagined, not romantic, but the actual feeling of a vast sense of space. Now, you will say, "Yes, I understand that intellectually." But receive that question entirely, with all your senses. Then you will find out if there is such a vast space—which is related to the universe.

Learning about oneself is infinite. Learning from books has certain limitations; all knowledge is limitation. There is no complete knowledge about anything. Even the scientists admit that. Outward knowledge is necessary and that same wave continues inwardly. The Greeks, and those before them, said "know yourself." That does not mean to go to somebody and find out about yourself. It means watch what you are doing, what you are thinking, your behavior, your words, your gestures, the way you talk, the way you eat. Watch! Not correct, not say this is right or wrong, just watch. And to watch there must be silence. In that watching there is learning; and when you are learning you become the teacher. So you are both the teacher and the disciple, and nobody else on earth. There is nobody outside who can free oneself, only one's own inward integrity, and having great humility so as to learn.

Love, Freedom, Goodness, Beauty Are One

WE ARE TALKING about the art of living. I think we ought to go much more into it. Most of us have given very little thought to it; we have hardly inquired into the nature of what life is and how to live our daily life with all its ugly turmoil, passing pleasures, and a great deal of entertainment, both religious and otherwise. We have studied academic subjects, spent years to become a doctor, a surgeon, or an engineer, and never at the end asked how to live a life without any conflict, without any of the problems that are involved in our daily unfortunate lives. We are always striving, reaching out, getting somewhere, and when a question, a challenge, is put before us, we say, "Yes, it sounds good, but tell me how to do it, what is the method, what is the system, so that we can live a life of great tranquillity, with a great sense of wonder, a sense of great beauty?"

I think we ought to banish "how" from our minds, not in the academic subjects, but in the psychological world. If one may most respectfully point out, never ask anybody how. They can only offer you a system, a method, which then becomes another bondage, another trap in which you are caught.

We have talked about wars. We have talked about how human beings are hurt psychologically from their childhood, hurt by their parents, by their schools, by their families. They are wounded people, and that wound inevitably breeds fear. We talked about fear a great deal. And we also talked about time, not only chronological time by the watch, but also time as a psychological means of achievement: "I am this, but I will be that," "I am violent, I will one day be nonviolent." This constant becoming from *what is* to what should be is also an element of time. Time is very important for us, not only physical time, to get from here to there, but also the ideal that thought has invented; to achieve an ideal also requires time. So we are bound to time. Writers and some other people have asked if there is an end to time, a stop to time.

Please kindly remember that we are investigating together deeply, seriously and with great honesty, how to live a life that is really a great art. So let's begin to inquire more. Humility is necessary to learn, isn't it? Humility, not humbleness, not a sense of remote acceptance; one needs a great deal of humility to learn. Most of us have not that quality of humility. It is not what you give to somebody whom you respect; that is not humility, that is merely acceptance of authority, and then you worship the authority.

Humility is necessary to understand the extraordinary complexity of living, humility with freedom. We think we are all very free to do what we want to do, to fulfill our desires. One of the structures of society is that each one of us is free to do exactly what he wants to do. You are all doing that. You want to be rich, you want to express yourself, you want to have your own particular way, you are very strong in your opinions, your conclusions. You are free to choose, and call this "freedom." Freedom has brought about great confusion, havoc in the world, each one expressing his own particular desire, competing.

What is freedom? Please ask this question of yourself. Is freedom a matter of choice? You are free to choose, free to go from here to there, free to have different kinds of jobs—if you don't like one you go to the other. You have freedom to express yourself, are free to think what you want and to express it, perhaps, in a democratic society. Not in totalitarian states—there freedom is denied.

So what is freedom? Does freedom really exist? Some of the root meaning of the word *freedom* is love. And is love a matter of choice? We ought to find out for ourselves what actual freedom is.

There is freedom *from* something, from pain, from anxiety. Is there freedom, not from something? If it is freedom from something, it is merely a reaction. It is like a man in prison saying, "I must get out of my prison." Psychologically, we live in a prison, and when it is painful, ugly, not satisfactory, then we want freedom from that. So we are saying that wanting freedom *from* something is the same thing as being in prison. What is that sense of deep, inward, authentic, unshakable freedom that is not *from* something? What is that freedom?

Let's together inquire into what freedom is. Everyone wants to escape from something. Most people are very lonely, and they want to escape from it through various forms of entertainment, religious and otherwise. But is there a freedom that is not a reaction? To find that out, one has to ask what love is. Is love a reaction? Is love attraction, whether it be sexual or otherwise? Please ask those questions of yourself to find the right answer.

How do you find the right answer to a question? When there is a question, you naturally reply to that question. If you are at all thinking, going along with the question, then you respond to that question. Then your response is answered. This is really dialogue. Then you respond to my response. So there is both question and answer, answer and question. If we maintain this answer, question, question, answer seriously, intensely, then in that process you disappear and the speaker disappears, and only the question remains. Then that very question has vitality. Test it out for yourself. It is like a rosebud; if the question is left in the air, as it were, then it is like a bud that gradually unfolds and shows its nature. The depth of a question has its own vitality, energy, drive. That is a dialogue, not just accepting what the other person is saying.

Is freedom that is not *from* something, love? And is love a reaction? For most of us, perhaps, love may not exist. Please, I am just asking this, I am not saying it does not exist. Perhaps most of us do not know what it means. We know attraction, we know tenderness, we know pity, we know guilt, remorse, and jealousy. Is all that love?

If it is not love, then love has no reaction. Then that is freedom, which is not born out of a reaction. . . . This is very important to understand, not intellectually, not verbally, but to see the depth and the beauty of it.

When we are talking about the art of living, we should also ask what beauty is. When you see great architecture, the cathedrals of Europe, the great temples and the mosques of the world, constructed by great architects, great painters, the great sculptors like Michelangelo, that is beauty. So is beauty man-made? Please exercise your brain to find out. A tiger is not man-made.

Thank the Lord! A tree in a field, alone, solitary, with all the dignity of a marvelous old tree, is not man-made. But the moment you paint that tree, that is man-made, and you admire it, go to a museum to see the tree painted by a great artist. So another part of the art of living is to understand the depth and the beauty of freedom, and the goodness of it. The aesthetic quality in life is born of sensitivity, is born out of all the senses in action, not one particular sense, but the whole movement of the senses. Surely beauty is when the self is not. When I am not, beauty is. When the self is not, love is.

And so love, freedom, goodness, beauty, are one, not separate. They are all interrelated. That word, *goodness,* is very old-fashioned. There is extraordinary depth to that word. The depth of goodness can be felt only when there is freedom, when there is love, beauty.

What is desire? What is the source of desire? Where does desire spring from? Is desire born from the object perceived? I see a beautiful car. Does the seeing create the desire? Please be careful; don't agree with what I am saying. We are going to contradict all that presently, so don't be caught in a trap. Does the object create desire? I see a beautiful house, and I say, "My god, I wish I had that."

We ought to inquire very carefully into what desire is. We are not saying to suppress desire, or give in to desire. We ought together to find out for ourselves, not be told, what desire is. You see an object, a car, or a woman, or a beautiful tree in a lovely garden, and you say, "My god, I wish I had a garden like that." Don't you know that kind of desire? You see something; then from that seeing there is sensation. From that sensation what takes place? Contact is part of sensation. If you have heard this before, don't repeat it, because then that means nothing. Seeing, contact, sensation—now, what takes place after that? Go very slowly, find out. I see a very good watch in the window. I go inside, examine it, touch it, feel it, feel the weight of it, see who made it. And then what happens? Then thought comes in, creates an image and says, "I wish I had it." That is, seeing, contact, sensation, then thought immediately creates the image; and then when thought creates the image of me having that watch, at that second desire is born.

Now, if you see that, can there be an interval

between seeing, contact, sensation? An interval before thought takes shape, makes a shape of it? Can you do it? It is all so rapid. When you slow it down, like a motion picture, then you see everything in detail. That is desire. So extend the gap. You are desire, you are the very structure of thought and desire. So if you understand, if you look into the nature of thought and your reactions, you can slow the whole mechanism down, so it is very quiet; or you understand this instantly.

That requires attention, that requires passion to find out.

If we understand the nature and the structure of desire, then we can find out what meditation is. Is conscious meditation, meditation? Obviously not. If I consciously sit down for twenty minutes in the morning, twenty minutes in the afternoon, twenty minutes in the evening, then it becomes a relaxation, a nice, comfortable, enjoyable siesta. So what is meditation? If you consciously meditate, it has a direction, a motive, a desire to achieve. Surely that is not meditation, is it? That is like a clerk becoming a manager. The two things are the same: you call one "business," the other you call "religious achievement," but both are exactly the same thing.

Do those who meditate see that? Of course not. That means giving up their pet enjoyment, pet entertainment.

We are saying that conscious meditation is not meditation because it is born of desire to achieve, to become something, which is the self becoming something, the self, the "me" becoming god. It sounds so silly. Forgive me for using that word. Then what is meditation? If it is not conscious meditation, then what is meditation? The word *meditation* means to ponder, to think over, and also to measure. That is part of the root meaning of *meditation* in Sanskrit. Now, can your brain stop measuring? I am this, I will be that. I am comparing myself with you—you are so beautiful, you have grace, you have brains, you have got quality, depth, you are wearing something extraordinary—and I am not that. That is measuring, which is comparison. Can you stop comparing? Don't agree. Stop comparing, and find out what it means to live without a movement of comparison.

So meditation is not a conscious, deliberate act. There is a totally different kind of meditation that has nothing whatsoever to do with thought and desire. And that means a brain that is really, if I may use the word, *empty.* Empty of all the things that thought, humankind, has made. And where there is space. Because freedom means that, love means that—space, vast, limitless space. And where there is space, there is silence and energy. If you are thinking about yourself all day long, which most of us are, then you have reduced the extraordinary capacity of the brain to such a small issue about yourself. Therefore you have no space.

The speaker is not a specialist on brains, but he has lived a long time studying by himself and watching others. The brain has its own rhythm that can be left alone. But when the brain is silent, not chattering, is utterly quiet, then there is that which is not measurable by words, that which is eternal, nameless.

So, you understand, love is not a reaction, therefore it is free. Where there is love there is intelligence not born out of thought. Intelligence is something outside the brain. Compassion, love, freedom is outside the brain. Because the brain is conditioned, it cannot contain this.

II

The Benediction
of Meditation

WHAT IS LIVING? Not what should living be, not what is the purpose of living, not what is the significance of living, not what is the principle upon which life should be based, not what is the goal of living, but actually what is living as it is now, as it is in our daily life? What is it actually in our private, secret daily life? Because that is the only fact, and all other things are unreal, illusory, theoretical. So what is this life, our life, the life of a private human being, the life of a human being in relationship with society, the society that people have made, which people have built. That society holds us prisoner. So we are the society, we are the world, and the world is not different from us. Which again is fairly obvious.

We are dealing not with abstractions, not with ideals, which are idiotic anyhow, but with what actually is, which is our living. What is our living? If you observe, from the moment we are born until we die it is a constant battle, constant struggle, with great pleasures, great fears, despair, loneliness, the utter lack of love, boredom, repetition, routine. Our life is the drudgery, the dullness, the boredom of spending forty years in an office or in a factory, being a housewife, the sexual pleasure, the jealousy, the envy, the failure of success and the worship of success. That is our daily tortured life, if you are at all serious and observe what actually is; but if you merely seek entertainment in different forms, whether it is in a church or on a football field, then such entertainment has its own pains, has its own problems. A superficial mind does escape through the church and through the football field because it is really not interested. Life is serious, and in that seriousness there is great laughter. And it is only the serious mind that is living, that can solve the immense problem of existence.

So our life as it is lived daily is a travail, and no one can deny it. And we don't know what to do about it. We want to find a way of living differently—at least, some of us say we must and make an attempt. Before making an attempt, before trying to change, we must understand what actually is, not what should be. We must actually take *what is* in our hands and look at it. And you cannot look at it, come into intimate contact with it, if you have an ideal, or if you are concerned with changing it. But if you are capable of looking at it as it is, then you will find there comes quite a different quality of change, and that is what we are going into now.

First see, actually—not shyly, or with reluctance, or with pain, or with resistance—what life is actually at this moment, every day. It is a travail. Can we look at it, can we live with it, be in intimate contact with it, be in direct relationship with it? Here comes the problem: to be directly in relation to something, there must be no image between you and the thing you observe.

The image is the word, the symbol, the memory of what it was yesterday, or a thousand yesterdays. That is, to put it very simply, the relationship that one has with one's wife or husband is a relationship based on an image—the image being accumulated through many years of pleasure, sex, nagging, dullness, repetition, domination, and so on. You have the image about her, and she has the image about you, and the contact between these two images is called "relationship." And obviously that is not relationship, but we have accepted it as relationship. So there is no direct contact with another human being.

In the same way, there is no direct contact with the actual, with *what is*. There is always the observer and the thing observed, and there is a division between them. It seems complex, but it is not if you listen quietly. And this division, or the screen in between, is the word, is the memory, is the space in which all conflict takes place. That space is the ego, is the "me." The "me" is the accumulated image, memory, thought of a thousand yesterdays, so there is no direct contact with *what is*. You either condemn *what is,* or rationalize *what is,* or accept it, or justify it, which are all verbalizations; and therefore there is no direct contact. And therefore there is no understanding and the resolution of *what is*.

I will explain this briefly and I hope it will be clear. One is conditioned to accept envy, envy being measurement, comparison. Someone is bright, intelligent, has success, been applauded, and the other, I, have not. Through comparison, through measurement, envy is cultivated from childhood. So there is envy as an object, as something outside of oneself, and one observes it, being envious. But envy is the observer; there is no division between the observer and the observed. The observer is the envy; and the observer cannot possibly do anything about envy because he is the cause and the effect, which is envy. So the *what is*, which is our daily life, with all its problems, fear, envy, jealousy, the utter despair, the loneliness, is not different from the observer who says, "I am lonely." The observer is lonely, the observer is envy, is fear. Therefore the observer cannot possibly do anything about *what is*. Which does not mean he accepts *what is*, which does not mean he is contented with *what is*. But when there is no conflict with *what is*, the conflict brought about through the division between the observer and the observed, when there is no resistance to *what is,* then you will find there is a complete transformation.

And that is meditation: to find out for yourself the whole structure and the nature of the observer, which is yourself. The observer is the observed, which is part of you. To realize the totality of this, the unity of this, is meditation in which there is no conflict whatsoever. And therefore, there is the dissolution, going beyond *what is.*

Then you will ask yourself: what is love? We are going to consider love together, though that word is heavily loaded, so trodden upon, so spoilt by the politician, by the priest, by every magazine that talks about it. What is love? Not what it should be, not what is the ideal, not the ultimate, but the love that we have, what is it? In the thing that we know, which we call "love," there is hate, jealousy, tremendous torture. We are not being cynical but merely observing actually *what is,* what the thing that we call love is. Is love hate? Is love jealousy? Is love possessiveness or the domination of the wife or the husband?

One says that one loves one's family, one's children. Do you love your children? If you loved your children with your heart, not with your shoddy little minds, do you think there would be a war tomorrow? If you loved your children, would you educate them to make them conform to a rotten society, train them, force them to accept the established order? If you really loved your children, would you allow them to be killed horribly in a war? As you observe all this, it indicates that there is no love at all. Love isn't sentiment, love isn't emotional nonsense. And above all, love isn't pleasure.

We must understand pleasure, because for us, love, sex and pleasure are involved. When we talk about love, we mean the enjoyment of sex, pleasure. And also it involves pain, torture. Please bear in mind that we are not denying pleasure. It is a pleasure to see lovely mountains lit by the setting sun, to see marvelous trees that have withstood fire, to see the dust of many months washed away by the rain, to see the stars. But to us that is not pleasure. What we are concerned with as pleasure is sensuous pleasure and the pleasure that we derive from something intellectual, emotional, and so on.

Pleasure, like fear, is engendered by thought. You have an experience of yesterday as you stood in a still valley, looking at all the marvel of the hills in that silence.

There was great delight and pleasure at the moment. Then thought comes in and says, how nice it would be to repeat it. Thinking about that experience of yesterday, whether it be the looking at the lovely tree and the sky and the hills, or thinking about the sex that you enjoyed last night, is pleasure. Thought thinking about that which gave a delight yesterday, thinking about it, living in thought, in image, is the beginning of pleasure. And you think about what might happen, about pleasure being denied tomorrow. You might lose your job, there might be an accident, ill health; thinking about it is pain, is fear.

So thought creates both fear and pleasure. To us love is thought, because love to us is pleasure, and pleasure is the outcome of thought, is nourished by thought. It is not the actual moment of seeing the sunset, or the sexual act, but thinking about it that is pleasure. So to us love is engendered by thought, nourished by thought, sustained and prolonged as pleasure by thought. When you look very closely, it is an obvious fact, not to be denied.

So, one asks: is love thought? Can thought cultivate love, or can it cultivate pleasure? It can cultivate pleasure, but it cannot possibly under any circumstances cultivate love, any more than thought can cultivate humility. So love is not pleasure. Love is not desire. But you cannot deny desire or pleasure. When you look at the world, at the beauty of a tree or the beauty of a face, there is great pleasure, enjoyment at the moment, but thought interferes and gives it a space and time to flourish as memory and pleasure. When you realize this, understand the structure and the nature of pleasure in relation to love—an understanding that is part of meditation—then you will find that love is something entirely different. Then you will really love your children, then you will really create a new world. When you know love, do what you will, there is no wrong. It is only when you are pursuing pleasure, as you are, that everything goes wrong.

Another problem is death. We have considered what actual, everyday living is. We have taken a journey deeply within ourselves to find out what love is, and we are also going to find out what death means. You will understand this really great problem if you know how to die. If you know how to die, then what lies beyond death, what happens after death, is irrelevant. So we are going to find out.

Death is inevitable. Any machinery, any organism that is being constantly used, will inevitably come to an end through old age, disease. Old age to us is a horror. I do not know if you have ever noticed how in the autumn a leaf falls from the tree, how beautiful it is, what lovely color, what gentleness it has, full of beauty, so easily destroyed. And with us, as we grow old, we look at ourselves, the pretensions, the disfigurement, the ugliness. Old age becomes a problem, because we have not lived rightly in our youth, in our middle age. We have never lived at all because we are frightened. We are frightened of living and frightened of dying. And as we grow old everything happens to us.

We are going to find out what it means to die, knowing that the organism comes to an end, and knowing that the mind, in its despair of coming to an end, will inevitably seek a hope, a comfort in some theory of resurrection or reincarnation. You know the whole of Asia is conditioned to accept that theory, reincarnation. They talk about it a great deal, write about it. They have invested their whole life in the hope of a new life in a next life. But they forget one final ultimate thing; that is, if you are going to be born in a next life, you must live this life rightly. Therefore it means it matters tremendously what you do in this life, how you live, what you do, what you think, how you talk, how your thoughts function. If you do not live rightly now, in a next life you would have the reward of not living rightly, which is punishment. But they forget all that, and talk about the beauty of reincarnation, justice, and all that trivial nonsense.

So we are not escaping from the fact through some theory, but facing the fact without fear. Knowing the organism comes to an end, what does it mean to die psychologically, inwardly? In dying, there is no argument; you cannot say, "Wait a few days more, please, I haven't finished my book; I haven't become the chief executive of some organization; I haven't become the archbishop, hold on a minute." You cannot argue. So one has to find out inwardly, psychologically, how to die; that is to end all the past, all the pleasures, the remembrance that you have cherished, the things that you hold on to. To die every day. Not in theory, but actually. To die to the pleasure that you had yesterday, which means die immediately to that pleasure, not give it a continuance. To live that way, so that the mind is always fresh, young and innocent, vulnerable, is meditation.

If you have laid the foundation of virtue, which is order in relationship, and when there is this quality of love and dying, which is all of life, then the mind becomes extraordinarily quiet, silent, naturally, not enforced through discipline, through control, through suppression. Then that silence is immensely rich. Beyond that, no word, no description is of any avail. Then the mind does not inquire into the absolute because it has no need to inquire. For in that silence there is that which is.

And the whole of this is the benediction of meditation.

12

Life Becomes an Extraordinary Thing

THERE IS THE ART of listening, there is the art of learning, there is the art of perception. The art of listening is not merely hearing words. Hearing the words is quite a different process from the art of listening. The art of listening implies that you are actually listening, not interpreting, not agreeing, not putting up resistance, but listening to what another has to say, so that you are not the translator of what is being said. You don't project your own conclusions, prejudices, opinions, judgments; you are actually listening. That requires a certain attention, and in that attention you as the listener disappear, there is just listening. When we listen attentively there is neither agreement nor nonagreement; we are just in a state of attention. Listen not only to what the speaker is saying but also listen to your wife or husband, which is much more difficult because you have become used to each other. But fortunately you don't know the speaker, the speaker doesn't know you, so we can both listen without any prejudices. It implies great sensitivity to have your senses active so that you are listening completely. If one listens so attentively, there is a certain miracle taking place. It is not a listening to one opinion against another opinion, or argument against another argument, however reasonable, however crooked, illusory, but a listening in which there is silence.

Listen so that you listen with your senses naturally, not just with the hearing of the ear but with all your senses awakened. Then you do not exist, only the sound. Sound has an extraordinary importance in life. There is the sound of the sea, the sound of the voice of your wife or husband, the sound among the leaves, the sound of the waves, the sound of a tree that is very still. Sound has extraordinary importance.

And there is the art of learning. The art of learning is not the accumulation of memory. You go to school where you cultivate memory, learn mathematics, biology, physics, and so on. You are being informed. Your brain is gathering information, storing knowledge about mathematics or geography, history, whatever you like, and that knowledge remains stored in the brain to be used skillfully or not skillfully in earning a livelihood. So knowledge is static. You can add to it, you can take away from it, but the core of it is static, it is not dynamic. That which is dynamic cannot be added to or taken away from, inherently it is dynamic; but knowledge is not. Knowledge is mere accumulation of information, storing the result of many experiences. That which is kept is not dynamic; that which is moving like a river is dynamic.

If you want to be an engineer, flier, or a physicist, you must accumulate knowledge; that is necessary, but it is adding to what is already known, so knowledge gradually becomes static. Whereas, in the act of learning you are moving, never remaining in the same place. Learning is the application now of what is being said and discovering for yourself whether it is true or false. If it is true, act.

In the world, theory and action (or life) have nothing to do with each other. You are full of theories, full of probabilities, possibilities; you say one thing, do another. You know the game you play. So learning is something that is whole, not fragmented as knowledge is. Learning is a movement like a river with tremendous volume moving.

Then there is the art of perception. Perception is different from seeing. Perception is not of time, but the seeing and the translating what has been seen into action involves a certain period of time. I see what I should do, and I will do it. Between the seeing and the doing, there is a gap, an interval, which is time. You see something that should be done and you think about it, you argue, probe, see whether it is convenient or not convenient, profitable or not, and so on. All that implies an interval of time before action. Whereas perception is seeing and doing so that there is no interval between action and perception. I see, I perceive that I should not be a Hindu because one of the reasons for being a

Hindu is for security, and also it is one of the causes of war. Nationalism, tribalism, is one of the causes of war. So I see that, I perceive it to be the truth and therefore I am no longer a Hindu. If you see the danger of being a Muslim, Hindu, Buddhist, Christian, and so on, you act instantly, as you act instantly when you see a cobra.

So there is the art of listening, the art of learning, and the art of perception. If one lives with this art, then life becomes an extraordinary thing. That requires great sensitivity, care, attention.

13

The Art of Dying

A S YOU ARE, most human beings throughout the world are afraid of death. That is one of the fundamental fears of life. We all know that death is for everybody, for you and me. That is an absolute certainty. You cannot escape from that. You might live longer by not wasting your energy, by leading a simple, sane, rational life; but whatever the way you live, death is inevitable. It is a fact.

Would you face that fact? You are going to die, so is the speaker. "You," who are you? Who are you, sirs, and ladies, who are you? You have money, you have position, you have capacity, you have dishonesty, your confusions, your anxiety, your loneliness, your bank account. You are all that, aren't you? Be simple and honest. It is so. And we are asking, what is the art of living when we are going to die? What is the art of living so that one is not afraid of death?

Let's go into it, not intellectually, not theoretically, but actually, so that you know what death means. We are not advocating suicide. There are certain philosophers, the existentialists and others, who say life is a perpetual going up the hill and coming down the hill, pushing up the hill, and after you reach a certain height coming down. They say that such a life has no meaning, therefore commit suicide. We are not saying that is the way to live. That is not the art of living. We are asking ourselves why we are afraid of death. Whether we are young, old, and so on, why is there this torment of which we are so afraid? It may be conscious or unconscious. And the fear of death is also suffering, suffering in leaving my family, suffering in leaving all the things I have accumulated.

So the art of living is not only to find out how to live our daily life, but also to find out what the significance of death is, while living. What is death? There is the biological, organic ending through disease, through old age, accident, through some misfortune. What do we mean by dying? If we can understand that, then life and death can live together; then death is not at the end when the organism ends, but you live with death and life together.

Ask that question. Put to yourself this question of whether it is possible to live, live the art of living, living with death. To find that out, you must find out what living is. Which is more important, living or dying, before or after? Most people are concerned with after, whether there is reincarnation, all that kind of stuff. But they never ask about the living, which is more important, which is an art. If there is right living, perhaps death is also part of right living, not at the end of one's stupid life.

So, what is living. We can discuss it, have a dialogue about it, but you have to answer that question for yourself. What is your life? What is your daily life, which is what your life is; it is a long series of daily lives. What are those lives? Pain, anxiety, insecurity, uncertainty, some kind of illusory devotion to some entity that we have invented, some kind of fanciful, illusory existence, a make-believe life, having faith, having belief. All that is what you are. You are attached to your house, to your money, to your bank, to your wife, children. You are attached; this is your life. You live a constant struggle, with constant effort, discomfort, pain, loneliness, sorrow. That is your life. And you are afraid to let that go. And death says, "My friend, you cannot take it with you." You cannot take your money, your family, your knowledge, your beliefs. Death says you have to leave all that behind. Would you agree, or do you deny that? Face it.

Death says to me, "When I come you have to let go." Now, is it possible for me, living, to let go? Will you let go? I am attached to my furniture. I have polished it, I have looked after it, I won't give it away; it is mine, it is part of me. When I am attached to a piece of furniture, that furniture is me. Death says, "My friend, you can't take that desk with you." So can you be totally free, totally free of attachment to that piece of furniture? That is death. So you are living and dying, all the time.

See the beauty of it. See the freedom that gives you, the energy, the capacity. When you are attached there is fear, there is anxiety, uncertainty, and uncertainty, fear, causes sorrow.

Sorrow is part of life. Everyone on earth has suffered, has shed tears. Haven't you shed tears? Your husband doesn't care for you, he uses you and you use him. And you suddenly realize how ugly that is, and you suffer. People have killed each other throughout history in the name of religion, in the name of god, in the name of nationality. So humanity has suffered immensely. And they have never been able to solve that problem, never solved suffering. Where there is suffering there is no love. In suffering there is not only self-pity, there is also fear of loneliness, of separation, of divisions. Remorse, guilt, all that is contained in that word, *suffering*. And we have never solved this problem. We put up with it, we shed tears and carry the memory of the son, the brother, the wife, or the husband for the rest of our life. Is there an end to sorrow? Or must we forever and ever carry this burden? To find that out is also the art of living. The art of living is to have no fear. And also the art of living is to have no sorrow.

One of the problems of life is to see whether it is possible to live without sorrow. What is sorrow? When my son dies, something has broken in me, especially if I am a woman. I have borne him in my womb, given birth, and I have nursed him, looked after him—and the pain of all that, the pleasure of it, the joy of the mother—and then he ends up being killed. For your country, he will be killed. Why do you allow it?

So what is sorrow? Is it that my son has gone, can never return? Though I think we will meet in a next life, he is gone. That is a fact. But I carry the memory, I keep his picture near my heart. I live on that memory, shedding tears, I cannot forget. It is part of my burden. We have never inquired into sorrow, into suffering, and asked whether it can ever end, not at the end of one's life, but now, today.

Is the cause of sorrow self-pity? Is it that my son was young, fresh, alive, and now is gone? Is it that I am attached to him? Face all this. What is that attachment? To whom am I attached? To my son? What do I mean by "my son"? Be rational, logical. What is my son? I have a picture of him, I have an image of him, I want him to be something. He is my son, and I am attached desperately because he will carry on my business, he will be better at getting more money. I also have a certain affection, we will not call it love, but we will call it a certain kind of affection. If you loved your son you would have a different kind of education, a different kind of upbringing, not just to follow in your footsteps. He is the new generation, and a new generation may be totally different from yours. I hope he is. I want him to be a new generation, of a different type of person than me. I want him to inherit my money, my possessions, my house. And when he dies, everything goes. How cruel all this is. And this is one of the causes of great sorrow.

And death, of course, is the final sorrow. But if you are living with death and life together, then there is no change. You are incarnating every day afresh—not "you," a new thing is incarnating every day afresh. And in that there is great beauty. That is creation. In that there is tremendous freedom. And the root meaning of the word *freedom* is love. The art of living and the art of dying, together, bring about great love. And love has its own intelligence, not the intelligence of a cunning mind. Intelligence is something outside of the brain.

14

Seeing Is the
Only Truth

IT IS VERY IMPORTANT to observe. It is quite an art, to which one must give a great deal of attention. We see only very partially, we never see anything completely, with the totality of our mind, or with the fullness of our heart. Unless we learn this extraordinary art, it seems to me that we shall be functioning, living, through a very small part of our mind, through a small segment of the brain.

For various reasons, we never see anything completely. Because we are so concerned with our own problems, or we are so conditioned, so heavily burdened with belief, with tradition, with the past, it actually prevents us from seeing or listening.

We never see a tree except through the image that we have of it, the concept of that tree; but the concept, the knowledge, the experience, is entirely different from the actual tree. Look at a tree and you will find how extraordinarily difficult it is to see it completely, so that no image, no screen, comes between the seeing and the actual fact. By completely I mean with the totality of your mind and heart, not a fragment of it. We are either emotional, sentimental, or very intellectual, which obviously prevents us from actually seeing the color, the beauty of the light, the trees, the birds. We never are in direct relationship with any of this.

I doubt very much if we are in relationship with anything, even with our own ideas, thoughts, motives, impressions; there is always the image that is observing, even when we observe ourselves.

It is very important to understand that the act of seeing is the only truth; there is nothing else. If I know how to see a tree, or a bird, or a lovely face, or the smile of a child, there it is, I don't have to do anything more. But that seeing of the bird, of the leaf, listening to the noise of birds, becomes almost impossible because of the image that one has built, not only about nature but also about others. These images actually prevent us from seeing and feeling, feeling being entirely different from sentimentality and emotion.

As we said, we see everything fragmentarily. We are trained from childhood to look, to observe, to learn, to live, in a fragment. And there is the vast expanse of the mind that we never touch or know. That mind is vast, immeasurable, but we never touch it; we do not know the quality of it because we have never looked at anything completely, with the totality of our mind, of our heart, of our nerves, of our eyes, of our ears. To us the word, the concept, is extraordinarily important, not the acts of seeing and doing. But conceptual living, that is, having the concept, which is a belief, an idea, prevents us from actually seeing, doing; and therefore we say we have problems of action, of what to do or not to do. Conflict arises between the act and the concept.

Do please observe what I am talking about, not merely hear the words, but observe yourselves, using the speaker as a mirror in which you can see yourself. What the speaker has to say is of very little importance, and the speaker himself is of no importance whatsoever, but what you gather out of observing yourself is important, because there must be a total revolution, a complete mutation in our minds, in our way of living, in our feeling, in the activities of our daily life. And to bring about such fundamental, deep revolution is possible only when you know how to look; because when you do look, you are looking not only with your eyes and nerves, but you are also seeing with your heart, with your mind. And you cannot see completely in this way if you are living, functioning, thinking, acting within a fragment of the total mind.

Look at what is happening in the world. We are being conditioned by society, by the culture in which we live, and that culture is the product of humanity. There is nothing holy, or divine, or eternal about culture. Culture, society, books, radios, all that we listen to and see, the many influences of which we are either conscious or unconscious, all these encourage us to live within a very small fragment of the vast field of the mind. You go through school, college, and learn a technique to earn a living; for the next forty or fifty years you spend your life, your time, your energy, your thought, in that specialized little field. There is the vast field of the mind, and unless we bring about a radical change in this fragmentation, there can be no revolution at all. There will be economic, social, and so-called cultural modifications, but human beings will go on suffering, will go on in conflict, in war, in misery, in sorrow, and in despair.

You can be a clever lawyer, a first-class engineer, or an artist, or a great scientist, but it is always within a fragment of the whole. Actually see what is taking place. The communists are doing it, the capitalists are doing it, parents, schools, education are all shaping the mind to function within a certain pattern, a certain fragment. And we are always concerned with bringing about a change only within the pattern, within the fragment.

How is one to realize this, not theoretically, not as a mere idea, but see the actuality of it, see the actual? The actual is what is taking place every day and is spoken of in newspapers, by politicians, through culture and tradition, in the family. When you see, you must question yourself. I am sure you would if you saw, and that is why it is very important to understand how you see. If you really saw the fragmentation, then the question would be, "How can the total mind act?" I do not mean the fragment, not the conditioned mind, nor the educated, sophisticated mind, the mind that is afraid, the mind that says, "There is God," or "There is no God"; "There is my family, your family, my nation, your nation."

Then you will ask how this totality of the mind can be, how it can function completely, even while learning a technique. It has to learn a technique and to live in relationship with others in our present disordered society. Bearing that in mind, one must ask the fundamental question, "How can this totality of the mind be made completely sensitive, so that even the fragment becomes sensitive?"

At present, we are not sensitive; there are spots in this field that are sensitive, but when our particular personality, our particular idiosyncrasy, or our particular pleasures are denied, then there is a battle. We are sensitive in fragments, in spots, but we are not sensitive completely. So the question is, how can the fragment, which is part of the total, which is being made dull every day by repetition, also be made sensitive as well as the total?

You may never have asked yourself about it, because we are all satisfied to live with as little trouble and conflict as possible in that little part of that field that is our life, appraising the marvelous culture of that little part as opposed to other cultures. We are not even aware what the implications are of living in a tiny fragment, a corner of a very vast field. We don't see for ourselves how deeply we are concerned with the little part, and we are trying to find answers to the problem within that fragment, within that little corner of this vast life. We ask ourselves how the mind, which is now half asleep in this vast field, because we are concerned only with the little part, can become totally aware of this whole thing, become completely sensitive.

There is no method, because any method, system, repetition, or habit, is essentially part of the corner of that field. The first thing is to see the actual fact of the little corner and what its demands are. Then we can ask how we can make the whole field completely sensitive, because in that lies the only true revolution. When there is total sensitivity of the whole of the mind, then we will act differently; our thinking, feeling, will be wholly of a different dimension. But there is no method. Don't ask, "How am I to arrive, achieve, become sensitive?" You cannot go to college to become sensitive; you cannot read books or be told what to do to become sensitive. This is what you have been doing within that corner of the field, and it has made you more and more insensitive. This can be seen in your daily life, with its callousness, brutality, and violence. We become callous because we are functioning, living, acting, within the small, petty little corner of a distorted field.

There is no method. Please do realize this, because when you realize it, you are free of the enormous weight of all authority, and so free of the past. The past is implicit in our culture, which we think is so wonderful—the traditions, the beliefs, the memories. All that is put aside completely, forever, when you realize there is no method of any kind to bring freedom from the "little corner." But you have to learn all about the little corner. Then you are free of the burden that makes you insensitive.

Now, as there is no method, what is one to

do? Method implies practice, dependence, your method, my method, one person's path and another's path. The problem is that we do not know the depth and the immensity of the mind. You can read about it. You can read the modern psychologists, or the ancient teachers who have talked about it. Distrust them, because it is you yourself who have to find out, not according to somebody else. We do not know the mind, we cannot have any concept about it. You cannot have any ideas, any opinions, any knowledge about it. So you are free from any supposition, from any theology.

So, once again, what is one to do? All that one has to do is to see. See the corner, the little house that one has built in a corner of a vast, immeasurable field, and is living there, fighting, quarreling, "improving." You know all that is going on there. See it!

That is why it is very important to understand what it means to see, because the moment there is conflict you belong to that isolated corner. Where there is seeing there is no conflict. That is why one has to learn from the very beginning— no, not from the beginning, but now—to see. Not tomorrow, because there is no tomorrow. It is only the search for pleasure, or fear, or pain that invents "tomorrow." Actually there is no tomorrow psychologically, but the brain, the mind, has invented time.

What one has to do is to see. You cannot see if you are not sensitive, and you are not sensitive if you have an image between you and the thing seen. Seeing is the act of love. You know what makes the total mind sensitive? Only love. You can learn a technique and yet love; but if you have technique and no love you are going to destroy the world. Do watch it in yourselves, do go into it in your own minds and hearts and you will see it for yourselves. Seeing, observing, listening are the greatest acts. If you are looking out from that little corner, you cannot see what is happening in the world—the despair, the anxiety, the aching loneliness, the tears of the mothers, wives, lovers, of those people who have been killed. You have to see all this, neither emotionally nor sentimentally, not saying, "I am against war," or "I am for war," because sentimentality and emotionalism are the most destructive things. They avoid facts and so avoid *what is*.

So, the seeing is all-important. The seeing is the understanding. You cannot understand through the mind, through the intellect, or understand through a fragment. There is understanding only when the mind is completely quiet, which means when there is no image.

Seeing destroys all barriers. As long as there is separation between you and the tree, between you and me, and between you and your neighbor—the neighbor a thousand miles away or next door—there must be conflict. Separation means conflict, that is very simple. And we have lived in conflict; we are used to conflict and to separation. India sees itself as a geographical, political, economical, social, cultural unit, and the same goes for Europe, and America, and Russia. They see separate units, each against the other, and all this separation is bound to breed war. This does not mean that we must all agree, or if we disagree, that I am doing battle with you. There is no disagreement whatsoever, or agreement, when you see something as it is. It is only when you have opinions about what you see that there is disagreement and that there is separation.

In seeing a tree, when you actually see it, there is no division between you and the tree, there is no observer seeing the tree. Observe for yourself a tree, a flower, the face of a person. Look at any one of them, and so look that the space between you and them is nonexistent. And you can only look that way when there is *love,* that word that has been so misused. When you have this sense of real observation, real seeing, then that seeing brings with it extraordinary elimination of time and space, which comes about when there is love. And you cannot have love without recognizing beauty. You may talk about beauty, write, design, but if you have no love, nothing is beautiful. Being without love means that you are not totally sensitive. And because you are not totally sensitive you are degenerating. You are degenerating because you are not sensitive to the whole process of living.

Our fundamental problem, then, is not how to stop wars, not which "God" is better, not which political system or economic system is better, not which party is worth voting for. The most fundamental problem for the human being, whether he is in America, India, Russia, or anywhere else, is this question of freedom from "the little corner." And that little corner is ourselves, that little corner is your shoddy little mind. We have made that little corner, because our own little minds are fragmented and therefore incapable of being sensitive to the whole. We want that little part to be made safe, peaceful, quiet, satisfying, pleasurable—thereby avoiding all pain, because, fundamentally, we are seeking pleasure. If you have examined pleasure, your own pleasure, have observed it, watched it, gone into it, you see that where there is pleasure, there is pain. You cannot have one without the other; and we are always demanding more pleasure and therefore inviting more pain. And on that we have built this part, which we call human life. Seeing is to be intimately in contact with it, and you cannot be intimately, actually in contact with it if you have concepts, beliefs, dogmas, or opinions.

So what is important is to see and to listen. Listen to the birds, listen to your wife's voice, however irritating, beautiful, or ugly. Listen to it and listen to your own voice, however beautiful, ugly, or impatient it may be. Then out of this listening you will find that all separation between the observer and the observed comes to an end. Therefore no conflict exists and you observe so carefully that the very observation is discipline; you do not have to impose discipline. And that is the beauty, if you only realize it; that is the beauty of seeing. If you can see, you have nothing else to do, because in that seeing there is all discipline, all virtue, which is attention.

And in that seeing there is all beauty, and with beauty there is love. Then when there is love you have nothing more to do. Then where you are, you have heaven; then all seeking comes to an end.

15

Life without a
Shadow of Control

WHAT PLACE HAS meditation in daily life? Or is meditation something separate from daily life? Is it an idea that you must meditate, that you must do this, that you must do that? Do you come to a conclusion and introduce that concept into daily life? Or do you try to find out what relationship action has with the total awareness of consciousness?

Why should one meditate at all? We lead our daily life rather unhappily, shoddily, in conflict, misery, suffering, deceived by others, and so on. That is our daily life. Why do we want to introduce meditation into that? Or is understanding the meaning, the structure, the reactions, of conflict, sorrow, arrogance, pride, and so on, part of meditation?

It is not that you meditate and then introduce it into action, into daily life, but rather that during daily life, when you go to the office, when you are working in the factory, or plowing a field, or talking to your wife, husband, girl, or boy, you are aware of your reactions. In the investigation and comprehension of those reactions—of why you are jealous, why a state of anxiety exists in you, why you accept authority, why you depend on another—that exploration itself is meditation. It is not the other way round, and it is not an intellectual understanding. If you meditate and then introduce what you think is meditation into daily life, there is conflict. You think this is so, and you are bringing that into action, into daily life, so there must be contradiction. Whereas if one is envious, as most of us are, seeing what the nature of envy is, why we are envious—not saying it is right or wrong, or that we should not be, or should be, but inquiring into why this envy arises and being free of it—is the movement of meditation. In that there is no conflict; you are inquiring constantly. This demands your attention; this demands that you must be serious, not just play with words.

So meditation has a place in daily life when there is an inquiry into the whole nature and structure of your being—your reactions, the state of your consciousness, why you believe, don't believe, why you are influenced by institutions, and so on. All that is an actual movement of meditation. If one is actually, not theoretically, doing it, then you begin to understand the nature of consciousness. You are not imposing something on it according to Freud, according to some psychologist, some guru. You are inquiring into your whole being; that being is your consciousness.

I wonder if you have ever inquired into the whole movement of thought, the whole activity of thinking, and whether thought, thinking, can see itself moving. Please, this is rather important if you want to go into it, if you are at all serious in this matter. It is really very important to comprehend the question first. I can say, "I am aware of my consciousness," through my belief, through my fears, through my pleasures, through my sorrow. I can be aware of the content of my consciousness by saying, "Yes, I am afraid, I am greedy, I suffer, I am arrogant, I have pride," and so on, which is the content of consciousness of which I am aware. In doing that, "I" am different from my consciousness.

So there is the "me," the observer observing his consciousness. But the "me" is greedy, the "me" is anxious, the "me" is frightened, the "me" is full of anxiety, uncertainty, sorrow, which is my consciousness, so I am not different from my consciousness. I am not different from what I think. I am not different from the experiences I have had. I am not different or something totally opposite to my anxieties, fears, and all the rest of it. I am all that. I may think I am God, but the very thinking is part of me, which invents God.

So then, if the observer is the observed, which is the consciousness, the question arises, can that consciousness be aware of its own movements? To put it very simply, is there an awareness of the arising of anger, anger itself, so that there is not "me" different from anger? Let's go into it. One is angry; at the moment of anger there is no recognition of being angry. Have you noticed? At the second, at the moment of intense anger there is only that state. A second later you call it "anger." Which means that you have recognized

147

from the past what has happened in the past, and what is happening now, and you say, "That is anger." At the moment of anger, there is no recognition and the naming of that reaction. A second later the naming begins. The naming is from the past; the naming is the recognition from the past of the present reaction. So can you not name the present reaction, but just observe without naming it? The moment you name it, you have recognized it and so strengthened the reaction. It is very interesting.

That is, the word is not the thing. The word *tent* is not the actual fact, but we are carried away by the word and not by the fact. So to comprehend, to see the fact that the word is not the thing is tremendously important. When there is anger, which is a reaction, to observe it without naming it so that reaction begins to wither away. The moment you name it you have strengthened it; the strengthening is from the past.

If that is clear, we can go the next step, which is, is it possible for the senses to be aware of themselves; not you are aware of the senses, but the senses themselves open? Kindly observe in yourself the reactions of the senses. Now our senses function separately, seeing, tasting, hearing, smelling, and so on. They are all separate. Is there a total movement of all the senses together? This is really quite fascinating to find out, because then you will see if there is an observation of a person, of the movement of the waters of the sea, of the mountains, the birds, or your friend, or your intimate person, with all the senses. Then there is no center from which you are observing.

Please do it, test it out. Do not accept anything. Test it out for yourself. When you smell something lovely, the perfume of an early morning when the air is clean, washed by the rain, and there is beauty in the land, is one particular sense awake, or are you observing the total delicacy and the beauty of the morning with all your senses?

Understand the sensory responses, whether the sensory responses are broken up, or the senses all respond together. If there is response of a particular sense, sensation, then what takes place? When there is only the reaction of a scent through the nose, then all the other senses are more or less in abeyance. Test it, test it out. I am asking if, when you smell a flower, there is total response of all the senses, not only smell but the whole organism responding with its senses?

When you hear noise, do you respond completely, so that there is no resistance to the noise, there is no irritation from the noise, so you are totally with the noise? Do you look at mountains, which you may have looked at every evening and every morning, not only with your eyes, optically, but is there a perception of the mountains with all your senses? If there is, there is no center from which you are looking. Test it out. Look as though you are looking with all your being, with all your senses. Then you will see that you are looking at something for the first time, not with jaded eyes and memory and so on.

So the question arises, can thought be aware of itself? You are thinking now, aren't you? When I ask you a question, the whole movement of thinking arises. Right? Obviously. Now I am asking whether that thinking itself sees itself thinking? No, it is not possible.

You see, I am asking whether one can live a life without having a single conflict, a single effort, without any form of control. We live with effort, we struggle; there is always achieving, moving, and so our life is lived in constant struggle, constant battle, constant contradiction—"I must do this, I must not do that, I must control myself, why should I control myself, that is old-fashioned, I will do what I want to do." All that is a movement of violence. We are asking if it is possible to live without any shadow of control. Which does not mean doing everything you want to do. That is too childish, because you cannot. Where there is control there is conflict, there is a battle going on, which expresses itself in many, many different ways—violence, suppression, neuroticism, and permissiveness.

So I am asking myself and you whether we can live a daily life without a shadow of control. To live that way, I have to find out who the controller is. Is the controller different from the controlled? If they are both the same, there is no need for control.

If I am jealous because you have everything and I have nothing, from that jealousy arises anger, hatred, envy, a sense of violence. I want to have all that you have, and if I can't get it I get bitter, angry, and all the rest follows. So can I live without jealousy, which means without comparison? Test it out. Can you live your daily life without comparing at all? Of course there is comparing when I choose something to wear. I am not talking about that. I am talking about not having any sense of measurement psychologically, which is comparison. If you have no measurement at all, will you decay, will you become a vegetable, do nothing, stagnate?

Because you are comparing, because you are struggling, you think you are living, but if you don't struggle, it may be a totally different form of living.

16

Is There Something Sacred?

THE ART OF LIVING is to have complete freedom, not the freedom of choice, not the freedom of what one wants to do, or likes to do, for that freedom is limited by the environment, by society, by religious doctrines, and so on. Freedom is something entirely different. It is not freedom about something or from something, but freedom per se. When there is that freedom, there is the supreme way of living without any conflict, without any problem. There is heightened intelligence when the brain is fully active, not active in a particular direction, either scientific or business, or with the problems of daily life. When there is that freedom, there is great energy, tremendous energy.

The word *freedom* also, etymologically, means love. Freedom implies inquiry into the problem of relationship. In that relationship, whether it is most intimate or with the neighbor of a thousand miles away, as long as there is an image about the person with whom you are related or he has an image about you, there must be conflict. . . . The whole idea of freedom as choice, movement, status, position, achievement, success, is only a very small part of freedom. It may perhaps be a most destructive freedom if everyone does what he likes, as is happening throughout the world. It will bring about great chaos, which is what is going on.

We have lived with conflict for generation upon generation, not only in our relationships, but with society, with other nations. Nationalism is tribal worship and that is causing enormous despair, wars, divisions: the Jew and the Arab, the Hindu and the Muslim, the communist, the socialist, and the so-called democrat. There is tremendous conflict going on in the world. This is the society that human beings have built.

Society is not something that comes out of the air. The society in which we live is created by every human being, and in that society, which is immoral, there is a great deal of injustice. One questions whether there is any justice at all. Society is what we have made of it, and we are caught by that thing we have made. Unless there is a radical mutation, change, a fundamental psychological revolution—not physical revolutions, which have led humanity nowhere—society will remain as it is now. Change implies time, change from this to that, change from violence to nonviolence. To change violence into nonviolence takes a long duration of time. Will time change human beings? That is a very basic, radical question. In time, which is an evolution of fifty thousand years or more, has humanity changed psychologically during that long period? Obviously we have not. We are very primitive people, quarreling with each other, with endless wars, always in conflict. Psychologically, inwardly, we have changed very, very little. Perhaps, technologically we have advanced immensely, with the atom bomb, telecommunications, the extraordinary development of machinery, computers, and so on, but inwardly, deeply, we remain what we have been for ten thousand or more years. Time does not change human beings.

Why are people frightened of death? As you get older, either you become a very religious, superstitious human being, or join some cult, or you begin to inquire into what death is, and why we have separated it from living, why we postpone it, put it far away. Why do we human beings do all this? Is it fear of losing the known, entering into the unknown?

Is it possible to live with death? Please, don't answer. You have to understand what living is. Living, as far as we know, is one constant travail, with occasional pleasure, occasional comfort, and if you have money you are more or less secure, but there is always insecurity threatening. Going to the office every day from nine to five, struggling, competing, quarreling, hating, loving (which is called pleasure)—all that is our way of living. That is what we know, and we are frightened to let that go. Death means the ending of all that, not only the organism coming to an end, but also all the attachments, all the knowledge, experience. So can one live with death and life together, not separate? Which means, can you live with death so that there is no attachment? Death is going to wipe away all your attachments: your family, your knowledge, your becoming, your fame, all that nonsense. Can we, as we live our daily life, live with death, which is to be free of attachment, of competition, of psychological becoming, so that there is no interval between living and dying? Then, you have tremendous freedom and energy. Not to do more mischief, not to get more money, to become famous, that is rather childish—forgive me. When you live with something that has immense meaning, that is freedom.

From the most ancient of times, humanity has sought something beyond the daily existence with its monotony, with its routine, its mechanical habits both physical and inward. Man has said that there must be something beyond all this. So he invented God. God is invented by thought. If there is no fear of any kind psychologically, absolutely no fear, not a shadow of it, not a breath of it, then is God necessary?

Man has sought this; and the priests came along and said, "We will interpret it for you; we will organize it for you, you are ignorant, but we are learned." And the process of that is to dress up in costumes, to impress, and also create a great deal of show. The ancient Egyptians, and further back the Sumerians, seven or eight thousand years ago, had hell and heaven too. They said you must believe, otherwise you will go to hell, and they persecuted, killed, tortured. Christianity has done this: you must believe in Jesus, or you are a heretic. Doubt is not allowed in the Christian world. If you doubt, then the thing collapses. But in the Asiatic world, especially in India, one of the teachings is that you must question, you must doubt not only your guru but question yourself, have a dialogue, never accept. There is no authority except the authority of the *truth*, not the truth invented by books or by thought or by priests.

What is religion? If you wipe away all the nonsense and superstitions and beliefs of organized modern religions, and not be a Hindu, a Buddhist, or a Christian, it does not mean that you become an atheist. It means you are inquiring, questioning, asking, discussing, pushing, driving, flowing.

Then, is there something sacred? Is there

something eternal that is beyond time? Is there something totally untouched by thought? Thought, the "you," cannot find out. Meditation is not just repeating some words; that is all too immature. Meditation is something extraordinary. Meditation is the understanding of the whole of life, both external and inward, the understanding of your daily life, your relationships, freeing yourself from fear, and questioning what the self, the "me," is. Is the "me" merely a bundle of memories and therefore has it no actuality? Please inquire into all this. That is all part of meditation.

The very word *meditation*, both in Sanskrit and in the ordinary dictionary, means to free the mind from all measurement, that is from becoming. "I am this, I will be that" is a measure. Measure is necessary for the whole technological world. Without measure we could not create a dynamo or the atom bomb, or build a car—but can we psychologically, inwardly, be free of all comparison, which is measurement? Can there be freedom from fear—from all the hurts that one has had from childhood, the psychological wounds that one keeps preciously, which distort our lives—freedom from sorrow, pain, loneliness, depression, anxiety? Can one be free of the self, the "me," not at the end of one's life, but right from the beginning, and right from the moment one hears this, live life?

Meditation means an extraordinary activity of the brain, not silencing the brain. When the brain is at its highest quality, full of energy, there is silence. Not the silence put together by thought, which is limited silence. In that silence that can come only when there is freedom, there is love and compassion with its intelligence. That intelligence is supreme. But there is no compassion or love if you are attached to some religious organization or belief in something. There must be complete freedom, and in that freedom there is a great, tremendous energy because there is an emptiness, not nothingness, emptiness. In that there is that which is beyond all time.

This is meditation. This is religion.

17

That Which Is Timeless

WHAT IS IT that one is seeking? I think it is very important to go into this because we are all saying we are seeking truth, love, and so on. How can you seek truth if your mind is not in order? Order is putting things where they belong, in their right place. When the mind is confused, uncertain, groping, unclear, wanting security, wanting something or other, that very desire, that very uncertainty, must inevitably create illusion, or a delusion to which you cling.

So one must go very carefully into what it is that human beings, you and I, are seeking. Is it that we want to be happy? Is it because we are so unhappy, miserable, in conflict, uncertain, neurotic, that we say, "Please tell us how to live a life in which there is happiness"? Is happiness the opposite of unhappiness? If you are unhappy, miserable, living in great pain and anxiety and suffering, you want the opposite of that: clarity, a sense of freedom, happiness, order. Is that what we are seeking? Please listen carefully. Is the opposite something totally different from its own opposite? Or does the opposite have its root in its own opposite? Man has *invented* the opposite. Not that there is not dark and light, woman and man, and all that, but psychologically, inwardly, the opposite that we want, which we seek, is the projection of *what is*. If I am unhappy, I want happiness. That is all I know. Caught in this unhappiness, the reaction is to have the other, happiness. That which I want is born out of what is actually going on. So the opposite has its root in *what actually is*. So the opposite has no meaning. What has meaning is *what is*. I do not know how to face *what is*, therefore I invent the opposite. If I know what to do with what is actually going on, then the opposite does not exist. So the understanding of *what is* is far more important than the pursuit of what should be, or the opposite of *what is*.

Why are we unhappy, miserable, quarreling, violent? Why are we like this? That is *what is*. If I know how to transform *what is,* then the whole problem is solved. Then I don't have to follow anybody. Then I am a light to myself. So is it possible to solve *what is* without wasting our energy in the battle of the opposites? It is possible only when you have total energy, which is not wasted in conflict. When I am unhappy, I have a sense of great anxiety. That is *what is.* To go away from that is a wasting of energy.

To understand *what actually is,* I must use all the energy that I have; then I can go beyond it.

Order is necessary in life. Order, as we said, means putting everything in its right place. But we do not know what the right place is. We only know disorder. There is disorder now: wars. Aren't you in disorder yourself, now, in daily life? Now, that is the fact, that is what is going on. And we want order. We think order is the opposite of that. That is, we establish a pattern of order out of disorder. We are disorderly in our conduct, in our thinking, in our behavior, in our outlook, and so on, and we think order is a blueprint of the opposite of *what is.* In bringing about order as a blueprint, there is always conflict. That is the contributory factor of disorder. Where there is conflict there is disorder, nationally, politically, religiously, in every direction.

So there is disorder. That is a fact. Now can you observe, be aware of that disorder? Not try to change it, not try to transform it, not try to suppress it, not say, "I must have order out of it," but just be totally aware of that disorder in your life. Then you will see that out of that disorder comes order, which is not the opposite.

Freedom from authority is absolutely necessary to find out if there is, or if there is not, ultimate truth. And freedom from belief of any kind is necessary, which implies no fear, because belief exists where there is fear, where there is despair. And there must be order. These three things. Then we can proceed to find out what meditation is.

What is meditation? Why should one meditate at all? Is meditation something totally unrelated to daily living? Is meditation something you practice? Is meditation doing something that somebody says, the meditation of a particular system, a daily practice, a goal, an end to be achieved?

You know what happens when you practice something over and over and over again; you become mechanical, your mind becomes dull, insensitive. Obviously. Isn't it so?

We think meditation is a process by which we can attain understanding, enlightenment, something beyond man's thought. This is generally what we mean by meditation. Have you practiced meditation? Have you practiced learning to control thought? Have you ever gone into the question of who the controller is? Who is the controller that is controlling thought? Is the controller different from the controlled? Or the controller is the controlled? You divide the controller and the controlled; and the controller then controls, tries to hold thought in a particular direction. But is the thought that wanders off different from the entity that is trying to control that thought? Aren't they both thought?

Meditation is to understand the proper place where thought belongs. Without control. Have you ever tried to live daily life without a single control? When you go into this question of meditation, you have to understand why man has developed this sense of controlling everything, controlling his thoughts, his desires, his pursuits. Why? And part of that is concentration. You know what happens when you concentrate; you build a wall of resistance within which you say, "I must concentrate on this," and therefore push everything else aside. Which is to exercise will to hold thought in a particular direction. And will is the expression, the essence of desire. And in concentration there is conflict going on. Your thought wanders off, all over the place, and you bring it back, and keep up this game.

You have never asked why thought should be controlled at all. The mind chatters endlessly. If you have an insight, if you see where thought belongs, then there is no problem of control of thought.

As there is no system, no practice, no control of thought, then you have to find out what it means to be attentive. What does it mean to attend? Attention implies an observation without the center. The center is the "me," my desire, my fulfillment, my anxiety. When you are attending, which means giving your nerves, your eyes, your ears, everything you have with total energy, in that attention there is no center as "me."

Now, just experiment with what is being said. Are you attending now? That is, are you listening completely? Listen! That means not interpreting, not translating, not trying to understand what is being said, but the act of total listening. If you are, there is only that sense of hearing without a single movement of thought.

You cannot go to a school to learn it. You cannot go to a college or university to become sensitive, can you? You find out in your daily life whether you are sensitive or not by observing, by seeing how you react to people. So, attention is necessary. And that is part of meditation.

Meditation also implies a mind that is totally quiet—not enforced quietness, because in that then there is conflict, isn't there? The mind is chattering, thinking, listening, going on; but you can see for yourself that a mind that is completely still can really observe. If you want to look at mountains, with their shadows, with their light, with their beauty and their depth, then you look, *totally*. When your mind goes off, that is inattention. But when you want to see something totally, completely, your mind naturally becomes quiet, doesn't it? So for a mind that is inquiring into something that is not put together by thought, there must be this total attention, and therefore complete silence, quietness.

Most of us find it terribly difficult, because physically we are never quiet; we are always doing something with our hands, with our feet, with our eyes. There is always something happening. We are never aware of our own body. If you are, then you will find that it has its own intelligence, not dictated by taste, by the tongue, by the imposed artificial desire for tobacco, for alcohol and drugs. A mind that is inquiring into reality, into truth, has to be totally free from authority, from all belief. That is complete order! A mind that is endlessly chattering, endlessly analyzing, endlessly inquiring, is wasting its energy; but a mind that is completely still regenerates itself.

As we said, meditation is to have a completely still mind, and it can only be still naturally, not be a cultivated stillness, a practiced stillness. If you practice stillness, it is death, it is no longer stillness. You have to come upon it. You cannot have stillness of mind if there is no compassion. So we have to go into the whole question of what love is. Is love pleasure? Is it desire? Can a person who is ambitious love? Can a man who is competitive love? Can a man or a woman love when he or she is self-centered? Or is love when the self is not? When I am "me" with all my problems, with my ambitions, with my greed, with my envy, with my desire to fulfill, to become something, or imagining that I am a great man, as long as I am concerned about myself, love cannot exist. Love implies complete compassion.

Out of that comes complete stillness of mind, because the mind has put everything in its right place, put everything where it belongs, so it establishes right relationship between man and woman, a relationship that is not based on images, memories, hurts. Out of that comes complete attention and silence.

And what is that silence? What takes place in that silence? Can it be verbalized? That silence is not a gap when there is no noise. A silence when there is no noise is not silence, like having peace between two wars is not peace. Suppose you have that exquisite, that extraordinary sense of the beauty of silence. What takes place when the mind is completely and totally silent? There is no movement of thought as time. There is no movement of thought as measurement.

Now I am going to say something that perhaps you will not like at all, because you are all very respectable people. When that silence takes place, there is space and absolutely nothing. There is space and absolutely nothing. See why it is important, because it is important to be nothing. Do you understand what I am saying? You are all somebodies. You all want to be something, either professionally, or you have delusions of grandeur; you want to achieve something or become something, realize something, fulfill. Which is all respectability. We are saying that in total silence, there is nothing, you are nothing. If you are something there is no silence, there is noise; and when there is noise you cannot hear or see. When there is nothing, there is complete stability. It is only when the mind is nothing that there is complete security, complete stability.

Only then can the mind find out if there is, or if there is not, something that is nameless, something that is beyond time. One has to live a life daily in which relationship with another has no conflict in it, because all relationship is life. If you do not know how to have a relationship with another without conflict, then life becomes distorted, ugly, painful, unreal.

All this is meditation. It is only then one comes upon that which is timeless.

SOURCES

7. THE ART OF LIVING
From the public question and answer session at Brockwood Park, England, 28 August 1984.

8. BE COMPLETELY FREE OF FEAR
From the public talk in Saanen, Switzerland, 14 July 1977.

9. ALL THE SENSES HIGHLY AWAKENED
From the public question and answer session in Ojai, California, 17 May 1983.

10. LOVE, FREEDOM, GOODNESS, BEAUTY ARE ONE
From the public talk in Bombay, India, 12 February 1984.

11. THE BENEDICTION OF MEDITATION
From the public talk at Claremont College, 17 November 1968, in J. Krishnamurti, *Talks with American Students* (Boston: Shambhala, 1988), pp. 122–30.

12. LIFE BECOMES AN EXTRAORDINARY THING
From the public talk in Madras, India, 7 January 1984.

13. THE ART OF DYING
From the public talk in Bombay, India, 11 February 1984.

14. SEEING IS THE ONLY TRUTH
From the public talk in Madras, India, 3 January 1968, in J. Krishnamurti, *The Awakening of*

Intelligence (London: Victor Gollancz Ltd, 1980), pp. 186–96.

15. LIFE WITHOUT A SHADOW OF CONTROL
From the public dialogue in Saanen, Switzerland, 28 July 1978.

16. IS THERE SOMETHING SACRED?
From the public talk in New York, New York, 15 April 1984.

17. THAT WHICH IS TIMELESS
From the public talk in Ojai, California, 20 April 1975.

BOOKS BY
J. KRISHNAMURTI

*Can Humanity Change?: J. Krishnamurti in Dialogue
with Buddhists*
Many have considered Buddhism to be the religion
closest in spirit to J. Krishnamurti's spiritual teaching—even though the great teacher was famous for
urging students to seek truth outside organized religion. This record of a historic encounter between
Krishnamurti and a group of Buddhist scholars pro-
vides a unique opportunity to see what the great
teacher had to say himself about Buddhist teachings.

*Facing a World in Crisis: What Life Teaches Us
in Challenging Times*
Facing a World in Crisis presents a selection of talks
that Krishnamurti gave on how to live and respond
to troubling and uncertain times. His message of
personal responsibility and the importance of con-
necting with the broader world is presented in a non-
sectarian and nonpolitical way. Direct and ultimately
life-affirming, this book will resonate with readers

looking for a new way to understand and find hope in challenging times.

Freedom, Love, and Action

In *Freedom, Love, and Action,* Krishnamurti points to a state of total awareness beyond mental processes. With his characteristic engaging, candid approach, Krishnamurti discusses such topics as the importance of setting the mind free from its own conditioning; the possibility of finding enlightenment in everyday activities; the inseparability of freedom, love, and action; and why it is best to love without attachment.

Inward Revolution: Bringing about Radical Change in the World

Here, J. Krishnamurti inquires with the reader into how remembering and dwelling on past events, both pleasurable and painful, give us a false sense of continuity, causing us to suffer. His instruction is to be attentive and clear in our perceptions and to meet the challenges of life directly in each new moment.

Meditations

This classic collection of brief excerpts from Krishnamurti's books and talks presents the essence of his teaching on meditation—a state of attention, beyond thought, that brings total freedom from authority and ambition, fears and separateness.

Talks with American Students

In 1968—a time when young Americans were intensely questioning the values of their society—Krishnamurti gave a series of talks to college students in the United States and Puerto Rico, exploring the true meaning of freedom and rebellion. Collected in this book, these lectures are perhaps even more compelling today, when both adults and young people are searching for the key to genuine change in our world.

This Light in Oneself: True Meditation

These selections present the core of Krishnamurti's teaching on meditation, taken from discussions with small groups, as well as from public talks to large audiences. His main theme is the essential need to look inward, to know ourselves, in order really to understand our own—and the world's—conflicts. He offers timeless insights into the source of true freedom and wisdom.

Where Can Peace Be Found?

Krishnamurti here teaches that the war and destruction human beings wreak on each other and the environment are caused by our misplaced attachment to a sense of self and individuality that leads to aggression, competition, greed, and conflict. When we recognize that our consciousness is not individual but common to all humans, we can work together in a spirit of cooperation and compassion. He also shows that taking personal responsibility for our actions and reactions—in our relationships and in our lives—is the necessary first step toward a global view.